Farmsteads
and
Old Neighborhoods

Tom Hintgen

Farmsteads and Old Neighborhoods

ISBN: 978-0-9981476-8-0

First Printing 2021
Copyright © 2021 by Tom Hintgen and
    Otter Tail County Historical Society

Published by J.O.Y. Publishing

Format/Design by Minion Editing & Design
www.joyminion.com

Cover: Barn painting by Scott Gunvaldson, Fergus Falls, MN

Printed in the United States of America by
Print & Mail Services - Otter Tail Power Company

Unless otherwise indicated, photos are courtesy of author.

Order additional copies:

Otter Tail County Historical Society
1110 Lincoln Avenue West
Fergus Falls, MN 56537

218.736.6038
www.otchs.org

Contents

Dedicated to my wife, Sharon, sons Mark and Paul, my sister Catherine, relatives, friends and to all who grew up on area farms and in Fergus Falls neighborhoods.

In memory of my parents, Roy and Claire, sister Mary, my in-laws Irvin and Delores Voigt, other relatives and friends, and the many people who grew up in the Fergus Falls area, no longer with us.

Introduction

Many of my former classmates in Fergus Falls have said that nothing compares to growing up on a farm. Other former classmates look back on the great times they had while growing up in city neighborhoods. These memories form the basis for this book.

Those who grew up on area farms refer to working alongside family members while milking cows, planting crops in the spring, harvesting in the fall, baling hay and doing other chores. They worked with animals from chickens to horses.

In rural Fergus Falls, and throughout Otter Tail County, life on the farm also included opportunities to watch the sunrises and see some beautiful sunsets. Many farm kids were surrounded by animals. Those kids loved country school, 4-H and friends on nearby farms.

Those who grew up in Fergus Falls neighborhoods and in other area towns, especially during the 1950s and 1960s, recall the days when they would collect empty pop bottles to take to the corner grocery store to cash in for a few cents in order to purchase penny candy.

Those also were the summer days of playing games: hopscotch on neighborhood sidewalks, kick the can, sandlot baseball, Anti I-Over and Starlight, Moonlight.

Kids also enjoyed swimming at places such as Pebble Lake and buying nickel ice cream cones at Dairy Queen or corner grocery stores.

John Runningen, who in an upcoming chapter recalls his days of growing up on West Summit Avenue in Fergus Falls and who now lives in Atlanta, Georgia, says he never forgot playing baseball on large vacant lots. 'We had to actually mow the fields before we could play," he recalls.

When kids got a little older, they would do some babysitting or help out with chores for neighbors in order to obtain some extra spending money. Getting into junior high was the time when kids earned money on the weekends, stocking shelves at corner grocery stores or sweeping out stores downtown.

Teens would drive back and forth through downtown Fergus Falls, circling between the Dairy Queen and A&W Root Beer on the south side of town and head to Dairyland on the north side of Fergus Falls.

It was a time when farm neighbors and residents in the communities would sit on front or back porches and actually engage in conversation. This held true for adults and kids alike while enjoying lemonade during the summer months.

"This was a time when all generations could sit together and actually communicate with each other," adds Runningen. "As kids we would learn the stories of our grandparents. We developed shared values and hopes for the future. Today, that's difficult – if not impossible – with so much usage of iPads and cell phones."

Country schools are fondly remembered, as are the many grade schools that kids attended in the various neighborhoods in Fergus Falls and other nearby communities.

At one time, Otter Tail County's 289 rural schools were the most of any county in Minnesota.

Many kids who grew up on farms formed their basis for life while attending one-room schools. City kids look back on the days when they learned the basics with reading, writing and arithmetic (the three Rs) at neighborhood elementary schools. And don't forget penmanship, particularly the Palmer method with rhythmic motions.

"Our teachers had the most beautiful handwriting before we had typewriters," notes Runningen. "Today that art may be gone, but is not forgotten."

Those who grew up on farms and in the community neighborhoods in the 1950s and 1960s also witnessed change.

Some of those changes are spelled out in a book, *Growing Up on a Minnesota Farm*, by Michael Cotter and Beverly Jackson.

"The small family farm started expanding," noted the authors. "There eventually was more competition for land, fence lines disappeared, the threshing ritual was replaced by combines, corn cribs gave way to corn dryers and hydraulic power replaced muscles."

Major changes have also taken place in the city neighborhoods. There were 23 neighborhood grocery stores in Fergus Falls during the 1950s and 1960s. Our community also had seven public grade schools. Those days are now gone.

One of the biggest changes from the 1950s and 1960s to today is the demise of many downtowns. And since then, we have witnessed the change from shopping at big box stores to shopping online.

Many former classmates who grew up on farms and who now live in big cities say they always have maintained some affection for the farm. The same feelings hold true for many former classmates who grew up in small town neighborhoods.

Even though I grew up in a Fergus Falls neighborhood, I also had the opportunity to get a taste of farm life through my friendship with classmate Bob Luther. I visited Bob often on his farm northwest of town, where his family had a dairy operation and grain farm.

I also took the opportunity, as a teenager, to do some pheasant hunting near the farm of Earl and Bessie Sharp, southwest of Everdell between Foxhome and Breckenridge. Their son-in-law was my cousin, Sonny Mjelde.

I have researched my great-grandparents, who farmed in the 1880s south of Mapleton, North Dakota. They were immigrants from Ireland who later operated a feed store in Fargo. Many times I reflect on the lives of John O'Reardon McAullife and Mary Catherine Williams McAuliffe.

Enjoy this book as people in their later years recall growing up on area farms and in city neighborhoods.

All book proceeds will go to the Otter Tail County Historical Society.

— Tom Hintgen

Prologue

AREA TOWNSHIPS IN THE FERGUS FALLS AREA

Fergus Falls Township, which shares its name with the city of Fergus Falls, was organized on June 29, 1870.

James Fergus, for whom the township and city were named, was born in Lanarkshire, Scotland, on October 8, 1813. At the age of 19 he came to America with the idea of improving his fortune.

He located in Canada at first, where he spent three years and learned the trade of millwright. In 1854, James Fergus moved to Little Falls.

Fergus furnished the necessary outfit for an expedition by Joseph Whitford, frontiersman. Whitford took an Indian as a guide and went to the place designated and staked off what is now Fergus Falls, incorporated in 1872, two years after Fergus Falls Township was organized.

Carlisle Township, west of Fergus Falls Township, was organized on February 24, 1881, and received the name of its village on the Great Northern railway, which was platted in December 1879. The village was named after John Carlisle, a

Kentucky state legislator who kept Kentucky from seceding during the Civil War and later became Secretary of Treasury under President Grover Cleveland. A city in England, a county in Kentucky, and villages and townships in 11 other states also bear the name of Carlisle.

Aurdal Township, east of Fergus Falls Township, was organized January 24, 1870. It was named for a village in Norway that is located between Bagn and Fagerness (about 105 miles northwest of Oslo).

Orwell township, southwest of Fergus Falls Township, was organized July 27, 1886, and had been previously known as West Buse, but was then called Liberty, which was changed November 3, 1886, to the present name. The name Orwell is borne also by townships and villages in Vermont, New York, Pennsylvania and Ohio.

Buse Township, south of Fergus Falls, was organized October 3, 1870. Ernest Buse, in whose honor the township was named, was one of the earliest settlers and became one of the most influential men of the county.

Born in 1836, Buse came to Minnesota in 1857 when his parents settled at Red Wing. He served in the Third Minnesota regiment during the Civil War (1864-65), and was the first homesteader on the site of Fergus Falls in 1869.

Dane Prairie Township, southeast of Fergus Falls Township, was organized May 10, 1870. The township received this name by choice of its people, nearly all being natives of Denmark. It has much timber and many lakes, with small intervening prairies.

Chapter One

Bjerkaas —
Both Farm and City Living

FARM LIVING

Carlton Bjerkaas, a 1966 graduate of Fergus Falls High School, lived on a farm on South Cascade until he was 10. The farm is now part of the Prairie Wetlands Learning Center.

Carlton Bjerkaas

"There were no kids our age near us," he said. "Life on the farm was mostly work. We had a large garden that needed tending and cows to get for milking. It seemed they were always at the furthest most point of the pasture."

Bjerkaas did have enjoyable times.

"My brothers and I played Ante-I-Over at the milk house and we also enjoyed the game of sticks. We rode our bikes to Madison School, even in the snow."

The Oliphants on south Cascade had quarter horses, but also dogs that used to chase the Bjerkaas kids when they rode past their house to and from school.

"Cascade was gravel until you hit West Channing – not great for bicycles," he said.

"In the winter we sledded down the hill in the pasture, dodging the trees on the way down. There was a barbed-wire fence at the bottom to help you stop. A slight challenge."

He trapped pocket gophers and cut off the front feet, taking them to the county agent south of where they lived to collect the bounty for them.

Bjerkaas spent time with classmate Steve Adelsman, who lived on East Alcott Avenue near Madison School.

"Steve had a room in his basement with lots of chemicals, much more than your standard chemistry set," Bjerkaas recalled. "I'm surprised we didn't blow something up, like his house."

He walked across the street to Bethel Church for Tuesday school. The building became the Broen Home and is now Alcott Manor.

"I believe I had the shortest walk of anyone," he said.

At Madison School kids played the normal games at recess: Pump-Pump-Pull-Away, dodgeball, kickball, etc.

"We had to be careful with kickball," Bjerkaas said. "The ball could roll faster down Sheridan Street toward Vernon Avenue than a kid could run."

CITY LIVING

Bjerkaas was 10 when his family moved from the farm to a home on West Bancroft Avenue, only two blocks from Adams school.

'I lived next door to classmate Roger Sampson," he said, "and across the street was my classmate Fred Huss until Fred moved with his family to the north side of town."

Another classmate who lived close by was Georgia Thaxton, who later moved with her family out of state.

"Several years later I saw her name in a UND (University of North Dakota) alumni magazine," Bjerkaas said. "She was living in Nebraska and I sent her an email. She replied and said she was surprised that someone from Fergus Falls remembered her. A small world."

Neighbor kids played the typical games – Ante- I-Over at the Bjerkaas garage, sticks and pickup baseball in the empty lot across from the alley. Players shared bats and gloves.

During the winter months, in the neighborhood near Adams School, Bjerkaas and his friends built snow forts and had snowball fights in the back yards. In the summer, they played "war" with plastic Army men in Roger Sampson's sandbox, sometimes shooing the cats away.

"Roger's dad was a World War II veteran," Bjerkaas said. "I recall him – all dressed up in his immaculate uniform, shiny helmet and spit-shined shoes with white laces – getting into his Ford and heading off to march in the parades as part of the honor guard. His shoes clicked when he walked. This was very impressive, especially to a young kid."

Brandon corner grocery store was a block from Adams school on Bancroft. It was always tempting for Bjerkaas and his friends to stop in and buy something on the way home from school. "And we did lots of window shopping," he added.

Bjerkaas walked to the various schools in Fergus Falls, first to Adams Elementary, then to Washington Junior High and finally to what was then known as Roosevelt Park High School.

Occasionally, he would catch a ride part way home from Roosevelt with classmate Rick Ronnevik in Rick's Plymouth.

Bjerkaas was a high school honor student, science club member, school annual editor-in-chief his senior year and an officer in the German Club.

UND and Air Force Career

Bjerkaas, after graduation from Fergus Falls High School, attended the University of North Dakota, majoring in Mathematics. He participated in the work study program, working in the chemistry department.

He was a member of the Air Force ROTC program and the Arnold Air Society. Bjerkaas received his commission in the Air Force upon graduation.

"My first assignment in the USAF was at San Jose State College, where I studied meteorology for a year," he said. "Following an assignment as a forecaster and weather briefer, I was assigned to Guam as part of the Typhoon Chasers."

He spent two years flying weather reconnaissance missions that included flying into tropical cyclones and typhoons in order to obtain location and storm strength information.

Bjerkaas participated in 21 typhoon penetration missions.

Carlton Bjerkaas, who was raised on both a farm and in the city, later made the U.S. Air Force his career. In this photo he is aboard a WC-130 in 1974, taking a weather observation.

left: "Typhoon Chasers" emblem (Public domain image courtesy of United States Air Force/Wikimedia Commons)

below: WC-130 (Public domain photo courtesy of United States Air Force/MSgt. Curt Eddings/ Wikimedia Commons)

"After attending graduate school, I was assigned to an Air Force research laboratory, conducting research with Doppler weather radar technology and developing automated storm detection and forecasting algorithms," he said.

Following attendance at a professional military school, he spent the next 13 years in various staff positions with several Air Force commands. Included was a two-year commander assignment in the Azores islands near Portugal.

The staff positions included duties as program manager for weather and space weather system acquisition, flight simulator and life support systems.

His largest program was NEXRAD, which was a joint government agency program to deploy a new national network of Doppler weather radars across the United States.

"My challenge was to develop a support program for upgrading and maintaining the network."

Bjerkaas retired with the rank of Colonel after 25 years in the USAF as the Director of Operations and Technology, Air Weather Service. His military service ran from 1970 to 1995. Two of the medals awarded to Bjerkaas from the Air Force were the Legion of Merit and the Air Medal. He was elected a Fellow in the American Meteorological Society, which is the professional meteorological organization.

PRIVATE INDUSTRY

Bjerkaas, switching to private industry after his Air Force career, relied on his more than 30 years of program management experience.

This included supervising technical program management personnel in activities ranging from the inception of system requirements, software design and development, system integration and database design.

In addition, there were assignments and leadership from Bjerkaas for installation of systems ranging from personal computers and workstations to mainframes, satellite sensing systems, operational tests and evaluation and chemical demilitarization.

In addition to his undergraduate degree from UND, he holds graduate degrees in Public Administration from Auburn University in Alabama and in Meteorology from the Massachusetts Institute of Technology.

THE WATER PUMPING WINDMILL

A landmark on many farmsteads over the years in Minnesota was the windmill.

Water-pumping windmills remained in use into the 1950s and 1960s at farms all across Otter Tail County. The water was used mainly for livestock.

A water-pumping windmill was simple and efficient. The blades of windmill wheels caught the wind, which turned the rotors.

At an individual water-pumping windmill, motion from catching the wind and turning the rotor drove a pump rod up and down inside of a pipe in the well. A cylinder with a sealed plunger going up and down inside forced the water up the pipe.

Each upstroke pulled water into the cylinder. On the downstroke a check valve kept the water from being pushed out, so the water was forced up the pipe with the next upstroke.

"I remember using our windmill for pumping water," said Hans Ronnevik, Fergus Falls High School Class of 1963, who grew up on a farm near Carlisle. "I believe we got

Windmill photo courtesy of Minnesota Historical Society

electricity about the time I was born, so growing up I recall being able to pump water with wind power."

If the wind quit, they could detach the rod on the windmill and hook up an electric pumpjack.

Adds Ronnevik, "I remember having Justin Kastet from Rothsay out to fix our well, and I think he also climbed the 60-foot windmill. He took care of any problems up on top."

Sometime through the years a strong wind must have damaged the Ronnevik windmill fan, so likely it was Justin Kastet who went up and removed the fan blades.

"Our windmill tower still stands," notes Ronnevik, "but the only thing left on top is the gearbox with the tail assembly, which now acts as a good windvane telling the direction of the wind."

Chapter Two

The Summit Gang

JOHN RUNNINGEN'S MEMORIES

John Runningen, a resident of West Summit Avenue in Fergus Falls, was in the Fergus Falls High School Class of 1971. The Runningen family, headed by Ray and Joan, lived at 1032 West Summit. Ray operated Runningen Café which later became Osterberg Café and then the Viking Café.

John has several good, detailed memories of West Summit Avenue, described in sections following his biographical sketch.

Joan and Ray Runningen with their children, Mary and John

After graduation from FFHS, John went to Luther College (English and Political Science majors) in Decorah, Iowa, through 1975.

"Then it was from the buckle on the Bible Belt to Sin City," John said.

It was at New Orleans and Tulane University where he received his MBA in 1977. John lived in New Orleans until 1988, when he moved to Memphis for 2½ years.

"This was from Jazz on Bourbon Street to Blues on Beale Street," he said, "and finally to Atlanta in 1991 where I have been ever since."

Runningen worked for a start-up hospital management company while in graduate school at Tulane, after a brief stint at Merrill Lynch where he learned to raise capital.

"I started a company to develop medical office buildings and healthcare facilities," he said, "and later was a healthcare research analyst at Morgan-Keegan and later at Robinson Humphrey in Atlanta."

Then he went into venture capital, where one of the companies was a start-up called *WebMD*.

"I worked for that company until the dot.com bubble burst," he noted, "and then started my own investment banking firm, www.CommendaCapital.com."

His focus has always been on healthcare companies.

THE WEST SUMMIT BASEBALL FIELD

As a kid growing up in the 1960s in Fergus Falls, John remembers the West Summit Avenue baseball field behind the Runningen, Engquist, Dideon and Hartl homes. The Runningen family provided the refreshments during those

John Runningen and his dog, Skipper

kids' baseball games, referred to by many across the country
as "sandlot baseball."

"We mowed it ourselves and made a covered dugout
on the west end of the field," John recalls, "so during late
afternoon we were not looking into the sun. Yes, we did think
of that."

"Only the players showed up. There were no fans," John
recalls.

He remembers that potential fans were on the next block playing kickball while their parents were at work.

OLD JOE, OLD JENNY AND OLD BROKEN DOWN

The woods at the end of West Summit Avenue in Fergus Falls, says John Runningen, had three anchor climbing trees: Old Joe, Old Jenny and Old Broken Down.

Old Joe was on the southwest corner by the dirt road overlooking Van Dyk Park, which today also is the location for the county historical society and museum.

Old Jenny was farther north by 150 yards and, according to John, was "the most superb climbing tree you have ever seen."

Old Broken Down, not to be confused with Broken Down Dam east of Fergus Falls, was on the west side of Summit Avenue. It was struck by lightning in the mid-1960s.

"It came tumbling down in the middle of the woods," John recalls. "On its side we could scurry up from the base and get into the limbs. When the leaves fell off, we could see and climb even further."

ACORN FIGHTS

There were lots of oak trees in the woods near West Summit Avenue.

"Needless to say, there were lots of acorns," Runningen recalls. "We filled dozens of grocery bags full to the top for acorn fights."

The kids had slingshots to shoot them across the street, or across the fields or whatever to keep the battles going.

"Needless to say, we learned to avoid windows after a few were broken in the numerous battles," John said.

He brings up the name of a neighbor kid, Al "Snudge" Hartl. The father of Al, Jr., "Snudge," was Al Hartl, Sr., the president of Otter Tail Power Company.

"I broke their kitchen window, just as all eight of them were sitting down for dinner," John said.

"My father made me walk over to the Hartl house and admit that I, along with my new slingshot, caused the damage. I of course said I would replace the broken window. Among the lessons learned during the early years of my life!"

A footnote: Al Hartl, Jr.'s, oldest sister, Marlene, picked the unusual name of "Snudge" for her younger brother after seeing the name in a book she was reading.

Just after his birth and coming home from the hospital with his mother, Marlene looked at him and said, "He looks just like Snudge." The name stuck.

KICK THE CAN

"Allie – Allie in Free" was what we would holler at the end of our nightly episodes of kick the can," recalls John. "With 63 kids in the neighborhood, we always had at least 10 to 12 kids ready to participate, usually at dusk."

They kicked a small tan plastic bucket in place at the Runningen front yard. John's parents were busy at the restaurant, and thus the least parental supervision and the most freedom for the kids.

"Our house was where all the kids in the neighborhood tended to congregate," John said.

For the boys, John had his fort, which was really a stump house or low-altitude tree house.

"Not to be outdone, my sister Mary had her playhouse for the girls," he says.

All of the kids, both boys and girls, could use the slide and the old Hintgen family (Cavour Avenue) swing set with monkey bars across the top.

If kids could stay over, they would hang blankets on the clothes line to make their own blanket-enclosed fort, with sleeping bags on the ground.

"Usually about 10 p.m. the dads would come searching for us, find us, and by then we were ready to go home to our own beds," John said.

Runningen says those were the things they did, for adventure, before the days of cable TV, the internet and social media.

FISHING AT PISGAH DAM

"Like all young boys, we liked to go fishing," says John Runningen. "To do that we had to walk through the woods, across Van Dyk Park and Highway 210 (West Lincoln Avenue), down the road past the packing plant, past the smelly rendering plant and through the sand pit to get to Pisgah Dam."

Today the dam is just west of the bridge that crosses the Otter Tail River near South Tower Road on the west side of Fergus Falls.

"Back then it was about a half-mile walk," John recalls.

Surprisingly, at 10 to 12 years of age they were given the absolute freedom to wander over there with fishing poles. When they arrived, the boys learned that the outlet just below the dam was the best fishing spot.

The Summit Gang at Marianne Fleming's birthday party
l-r: Billy Williams, Marianne Fleming (wearing crown), Pete Swenson, Jane Meyer, Meg Atkinson, Mary Runningen, John Runningen, Brand Windmiller and Jeff (Bobo) Skogmo

"It was a river where you would expect fast-water fish – but no, just sunnies and crappies," John says.

In the fishing gang with Runningen were Billy Williams, Bobo Skogmo, Snudge Hartl, and Peter and Paul Swenson.

"Most of us couldn't catch a thing. We didn't have the patience," John says. "But the one kid in our group who always caught fish every time was Pete Swenson. He still does today, 55 years later."

Ironically, Pete was and still is allergic to freshwater fish. But he can eat saltwater fish.

"Oftentimes Pete would catch a bunch of sunfish and take them home. His mother, Gen, would make Pete clean the fish himself. Then she'd fry them up and all us kids were given samples. Yummy."

STREET CLEANING

When Snudge Hartl and John Runningen were bored, they would sit on the curb waiting for something to happen.

"The biggest activity was when the monster street cleaner with brushes, came down the street," says John. "Our moms were sure we would get swept up, but we never did."

The big city-owned unit became a service model for the younger kids.

"Snudge and I put a 55-gallon soap drum on the back of a big red wagon with a small spigot over the back edge," John recalls. "We filled it with water, opened the tap and pulled it down the street. It was our own street cleaner."

Runningen says this was their first attempt at public service, based on what they had seen and then reproduced in their own right.

REGGIE THE ST. BERNARD

Snudge Hartl was the last kid in the neighborhood to get his own dog.

"And that dog was huge. It was a St. Bernard named Reggie," remembers John Runningen.

Reggie the dog slept in the Hartl garage in an old refrigerator box. He never came inside the house. Ruth Hartl was meticulous in every way, so that would never happen.

When the family was out of town, Reggie was boarded at a kennel south of town.

Once in the late 1960s, Al Hartl, Sr., went to pick up Reggie and was walking him back to the car. Then the unexpected happened.

"Reggie spotted a squirrel and, bam, took off," John describes. "He pulled Al, Sr., to the ground, dragged him over the gravel driveway to the kennel, scraped up his face and nearly dislocated his right arm."

Al, Sr., already had back problems, the result of military service during World War II. This mishap with the dog really added to his pain.

"Needless to say, Al had a lot of explaining to do when he arrived for work the next day at Otter Tail Power Company with a scraped-up face," John says. "But he gave the story straight and to the point on what took place, and then went about his business."

MOM'S BRIDGE PLAYING AND COFFEE PARTIES

Mae Fleming, who lived on West Summit Avenue, was respected throughout Fergus Falls as a former dancer and teacher. Her specialty was ballet. She also was known as "the queen of playing Bridge."

Every week Mae would host Dorothy Emerson, Ruth Hartl, Gen Swenson on occasion, and other women from around town.

Three or four card tables were set up, and from 8 to 12 ladies would play Bridge.

"The Catholic Church was well represented," says John Runningen. "Lutherans were there, but they weren't very good gamblers."

Adds John, "They had a ball and a much-needed break from chasing children. As I grew older, I appreciated their need to get away, if only for an afternoon to have fun. Today we have social media."

A footnote: In the late 1960s Mae Fleming choreographed and coached students in dance routines for many plays and skits at the junior and senior high schools and also at the junior college.

"Through Mae's guidance we became pretty good dancers," John Runningen says.

In 1966-67, Runningen and other eighth graders dressed up in all-white long underwear with bright red rubber gloves on their feet to learn the Chicken Dance for an eighth grade skit. The others included Brek Crow, Craig Smedstad, Tim Devorak and Jim Morstad.

The boys were accompanied by an all-girls rock band, consisting of Marianne Fleming, Julie Schwankl, Dana Gust and Becky Olderr.

Chapter Three

West Summit Neighborhood

West Summit

I remember the combined 900 and 1000 block of West Summit Avenue in Fergus Falls, known for its wide array of Christmas lights in the 1950s and 1960s.

Our family, consisting of me, parents Roy and Claire Hintgen, and sisters Catherine and Mary, knew many people who lived on this long block. We lived just to the south at 930 West Cavour Avenue.

Our back yard abutted the back yards of the Ward and Margaret Shaver family at 919 West Summit and the property of Flynn and Tillie Olson at 933 West Summit. It was woods behind our house in the early 1950s, when Flynn and Tillie built their new home.

Children of Ward and Margaret Shaver were Jim, David, Roger and Robert.

Merle Atkinson, who lived at 922 West Summit, was a Boy Scout leader for Grace United Methodist Church. Merle, who worked for Central Bi-Products, led a large group of boys comprising an elite group of Boy Scouts in Fergus Falls.

The children of Merle and Marion were Tim, Beth and Meg.

Arnie and Ann Skogmo, 940 West Summit, were widely known as the owners of the Skogmo Café. I was a classmate of Tim Skogmo. Tim's brothers were Jerry and Jeff, whose nickname was Bobo.

Bob Fleming, 1007 West Summit, owned a plumbing business, Fergus Plumbing & Heating. David Fleming was also a classmate of mine. David's siblings, children of Bob and Mae, were Roger, Marianne and Paul

Dr. Glenn Mouritsen and wife Virginia lived at 907 West Summit, in a house that they built. Their son, Jack, and my sister, Catherine Hintgen, were both in the FFHS Class of 1957. Jack's younger sister was Julie, FFHS Class of 1967.

Al Hartl of 950 West Summit was president of Otter Tail Power Company. He was a member of Our Lady of Victory Catholic Church, and was a neighbor to the Hintgen family who lived just to the south on West Cavour Avenue. Catherine Hintgen, Jack Mouritsen and Kathy Hartl were high school classmates.

The children of Al and Ruth Hartl were Marlene, Claudeen, Kathy, Mary, Pat and Albert, Jr.

OTP Safety Director Bud Poole and his wife Annette of 906 West Summit had a daughter, Nancy, who was in Blue Birds with my sister, Mary Hintgen.

Les Leitte of 910 West Summit operated Les' Tire Service (including bike sales), and was known as an avid horseshoe participant. A son, Steve, later operated Steve's Cycle & Marine.

l-r: John Runningen, Nicole Runningen (13), Jacqueline Runningen (10, seated, holding Skipper), Michele Runningen and Merle Atkinson seated behind the wheel with Tippy

L.L. (Red) Campbell of 1001 West Summit was a small appliance repair man at Hintgen-Karst, owned by my father Roy, uncle Ray Hintgen and Ed Karst in downtown Fergus Falls.

Bob Emerson of 1027 West Summit was a pharmacist, and with Al Stemsrud operated Stem & Em Drug Store in downtown Fergus Falls. Bob and Dorothy had two children, Steve and Linda.

Frank O'Meara of 911 West Summit operated O'Meara's Department Store. Dennis, the son of Frank and Doris O'Meara, was a classmate of mine. Dennis had a brother, Patrick.

Margaret Bjorklund of 915 West Summit was another friend of Mary Hintgen. Her parents were Vernon and Irene (Runningen), who prepared most of the baked goods for Runningen Café.

My parents, Roy and Claire Hintgen, along with me and my sisters Catherine and Mary, enjoyed dining at the Runningen Café, which in later years became the Osterberg Café and then the Viking Café.

The Runningen family, headed by Ray and Joan, lived at 1032 West Summit. Their children were John and Mary. The Runningens obtained a used swing set from the Hintgen family.

John was proud of their two dogs: Skipper, a Beagle mix and Tippy, a black Cocker Spaniel.

My sister Mary did babysitting for twins Peter and Paul Swenson, whose parents, John and Genevieve, resided at 1039 West Summit.

WEST SUMMIT AVENUE ADDRESSES

(in order of location)

902 – E.J. and Stella Halverson: they both worked in the Fergus Falls public school system; she taught sixth grade at McKinley School; they had two children, with son Bruce later working in the clothing business.

903 – Carl and Ann Lund: Carl was a physician at Lake Region Hospital; they had four children.

906 – Bud and Annette Poole: Bud was safety director for Otter Tail Power Company; Nancy was their daughter.

907 – Glenn and Virginia Mouritsen: Glen was a physician; their children were Jack and Julie.

910 - Les and Juline Leitte: Les owned Les' Tire Service; they had three children.

911 – Frank and Doris O'Meara: Frank was a co-owner of O'Meara's Department Store; their children were Dennis and Patrick.

912 – Forest and Ione Dahl: Forrest owned Dahl Music in downtown Fergus Falls; they had three sons.

915 – Vernon and Irene (Runningen) Bjorklund: Irene prepared many of the pies and baked goods for Runningen Café in her home and delivered them to the restaurant; their daughter was Margaret (Margie).

918 – Jim and Beth Mayer: Jim was an Air Force veteran from World War II; their three children were Gary, Jane and Kristi.

919 – Ward and Margaret Shaver: Ward was a radiologist at Lake Region Hospital; their children were Jim, Bruce, Rodger and Bobby.

922 – Merle and Marion "Tot" Atkinson: Merle worked for Central Bi-Products; their children were Tim, Beth and Meg.

933 – Flynn and Tillie Olson: Flynn worked at Ford Auto Sales.

940 – Arnie and Ann Skogmo: they operated Skogmo Café in downtown Fergus Falls; their children were Tim, Jerry and Jeff.

Jim Mayer with daughter Jane at her wedding

943 – Hylda Isaacson: she was a school principal at Lincoln Elementary.

946 – Myrtle Carlson: she was a retiree in 1960s.

950 – Al and Ruth Hartl: Al was president of Otter Tail Power Company; their children were Marlene, Claudeen, Kathleen, Mary, Pat and Al, Jr.

1001 – Red and Ruth Campbell: Red worked as small appliance technician at Hintgen-Karst.

1002 – Dr. Roy and Susan Dideon Nelson: Roy was a physician and Susan was a nursing assistant.

1007 – Bob and Mae Fleming: Bob was the owner of Fergus Plumbing & Heating; their children were Roger, David, Marianne and Paul.

1018 – Hillman and Agnes Engquist: Hillman worked as an agricultural instructor for the Fergus Falls Public Schools system and Agnes was an Algebra teacher; they had a daughter, Marilyn.

1023 – Roger and Elsa Gene Hegman: they both worked for the Fergus Falls State Hospital (later known as the Regional Treatment Center) in administration.

1027 – Bob and Dorothy Emerson: Bob was a co-owner of Stemsrud & Emerson Drug Store; children were Steve and Linda.

1032 – Ray and Joan Runningen: Ray operated Runningen Café, which later became Osterberg Café and then the Viking Café; children were John and Mary.

1039 - John and Genevieve Swenson: John operated Swenson & Sons Farms; their children were Peter, Paul and Lisa.

1040 – Earl and Dorothy Williams: Earl was an attorney; their children were Jimmy, Kirk, Billy and Elizabeth.

SPECIAL REMEMBRANCES ALONG WEST SUMMIT AVENUE

Steve Emerson told me that he remembers hunting pheasants at what later became the site for Fergus Falls

Community College, just north of the far western end of West Summit Avenue. Pheasants were located in a slough area.

Steve Leitte recalls his father, Les, as an avid horseshoe participant. A neighbor who had a lighted horseshoe pit was his friend Elmer Stanghelle, who lived on the next block east at 823 West Summit.

Steve later operated Steve's Cycle & Marine in a building that earlier was a 7-Up plant on the north side of town, just west of Dairyland and across the road from the State Hospital (Regional Treatment Center).

Kirk Williams had a Shetland pony in his back yard in 1957, a short distance from a location that later became the football field for Fergus Falls Community College. I was near his house when the pony arrived in the later 1950s.

Roger Fleming was a member of ROTC at the University of North Dakota; he served as a helicopter pilot in Vietnam, and sadly died in a private plane crash 40 miles east of Pittsburgh at the age of 40 in 1985.

THE STORY OF AL HARTL, A WEST SUMMIT RESIDENT

In 1941, future Otter Tail Power Company President Albert V. Hartl was a reserve officer in the United States Army. He was called to active duty to serve with the 7th Infantry Division in the Pacific Theater of Operations during World War II.

Hartl was featured in an article in the November 1943 *Readers Digest* on the invasion of Attu in the Aleutian Islands on May 11 of that year.

Hartl served as president of OTP from 1961 to 1975.

By the end of World War II, Hartl was a colonel commanding a regiment.

"His service record was outstanding," said the late Otter Tail County military historian Myron Broschat, also a World War II veteran who worked for Otter Tail Power. "Hartl won two silver stars and two bronze stars for heroism and one bronze star for merit."

Lieutenant Colonel Hartl commanded the small invasion force which landed on the north side of Attu in the Aleutian Islands.

The Al Hartl, Sr., family
front l-r: Al, Sr., Ruth, Mary and Pat
back l-r: Marlene, Claudeen, Kathleen and Al, Jr. (Snudge)

His command comprised of one battalion of the 17th Infantry Regiment, reinforced by a battery of artillery and support troops. These units landed to the west of Holtz Bay, taking a dominant terrain called Hill X. They later advanced to the interior to meet the southern force. A provisional battalion consisting of the 7th Scout Company and a reconnaissance platoon landed farther east to add additional strength to the northern forces' drive inland.

Although his men had to scale a 250-foot cliff and came under fire from Japanese 75-mm dual-purpose guns, Hartl moved quickly to capture his objective. A fierce Japanese nighttime counterattack failed to dislodge the Americans from Hill X.

"At officers' meetings Hartl covered everything, almost like a school teacher," wrote the author of the 1943 *Readers Digest* article.

Hartl, Otter Tail Power Company's fourth president, was born on Oct. 21, 1911, on a farm near Bremen, N.D. In 1932, he graduated from the University of North Dakota with a degree in commerce.

After graduation he was employed by the State of North Dakota in Bismarck. There he became head of the State Income Tax Division and later chief accountant for the Public Service Commission.

After World War II, Hartl joined Otter Tail Power Company in 1946. He started as the comptroller, advancing into upper management and in April 1961 succeeded Cyrus Wright as president of the company. In 1975, he handed over the presidency to Bob Bigwood and was elected chairman of the board. Hartl continued as board chairman until 1982.

"Hartl is best remembered for his organizational skills," said Broschat, "which reflected his military experience. Under his guidance, the company operated like a well-oiled machine."

Hartl was active in Boys Scouts for 60 years at various levels. He was president of the Red River Valley Council and received the coveted silver beaver, silver buffalo and silver antelope awards for his many years of leadership and service. He was an active member and leader in the Knights of Columbus. Hartl organized a new council in Fergus Falls, where he served as Charter Grand Knight. He later became district deputy and served as an officer of the state council for two years.

Hartl and his wife, Ruth, had five daughters and one son. He died on January 9, 1995, in Bismarck at the age of 83.

JERRY SKOGMO, THE STAR WEST SUMMIT ATHLETE

West Summit Avenue resident Jerry Skogmo grew up with brothers Tim and Jeff, the sons of Arnie and Ann Skogmo who owned and operated Skogmo Café in downtown Fergus Falls.

Jerry established himself in Otter athletics, graduating in 1968. He starred in football, basketball and track. He won the shot put competition as a senior at the state track meet.

Jerry was ahead of his time in physical fitness, lifting weights and keeping a disciplined schedule many years before weight training became commonplace in high school athletics.

After high school he starred in football and track at the University of North Dakota in Grand Forks. Skogmo later worked for a mental health center near Chicago.

In 1986 he became a charter member of the Fergus Falls Area Chamber of Commerce Sports Hall of Fame.

Jerry Skogmo was a star Otter athlete who grew up on West Summit Avenue.

Chapter Four

Luther Farm

LUTHER FARM MEMORIES

The Luther farm, a century farm about four miles northwest of Fergus Falls and near the junction of I-94 and Highway 59, has been owned by the Luther family since 1880.

The farm once occupied by Leonard and Eleanor Luther and their four children is located northwest of Fergus Falls.
The farmstead, still family owned, is near the Pelican River, southwest of the junction of Interstate 94 and Highway 59.

The late Leonard Luther, the third-generation owner, was born on the family farm in 1916. He lived on the farm nearly his entire life and owned the farm from 1947 until his passing in 2010 at the age of 93.

Over the years, the Luthers had a dairy herd and worked the land as grain farmers.

The land, now owned by Leonard's descendants, has been rented out since 1986.

The Luther Farm homestead

Christian Luther and his wife, Sophie, immigrated to the United States from Germany in the summer of 1880 with an infant son, Christian, Jr.

That same year they purchased the Luther farm, near the Pelican River, and began operating it as a grain and dairy farm. A second son, Henry, was born there in 1882.

"The trunk used by them to travel from their home in Germany to Fergus Falls, by way of New York, has been restored and is a treasured family possession," said Dick Luther, son of Leonard Luther and his wife, Eleanor.

Christian Luther, 40, died in 1891 while working on the farm. His wife Sophie continued to own and operate the farm with her two young sons. When they became young men, she told them she would turn over the farm to the first one of them to marry.

Henry, the second-born son, met Karolina Haarstick, who in 1911 lived about three miles east of the Luther farm. They were married in May 1912, one month before Henry's older brother Christian married.

As promised, Sophie transferred the farm ownership to Henry shortly after his marriage. Henry and Karolina had five children: Alvina, Harold, Leonard, Edwin and Henry, Jr.

The Luther children attended School District 96, which later became District 1434, not far from where in 2021 the ethanol plant is located.

The elder Henry died in the influenza pandemic in 1918 at the age of 36. His son, Edwin, and his brother's wife also died of the pandemic during the same year.

Karolina continued to own and operate the farm with her four surviving children. When the United States entered

World War II, three of her children (Alvina, Harold and Henry) enlisted in the Armed Forces. That left Leonard to operate the farm for the Luther family.

After the end of World War II, Karolina sold the farm to Leonard, who had married Eleanor Svenneby of Fergus Falls in 1943. They had four children, Dick, Bill, Lois and Bob.

Dick, the oldest of the children, said, "It's hard to imagine today the hard work that was required by our entire family

The Luther Family in 1957
Front: Eleanor and Leonard Luther
Back, l-r: Lois, Dick, Bill and Bob Luther

and all farm families back then. But it gave us all the work ethic and a good start in life."

Leonard and Eleanor operated and expanded the grain and dairy farm over a span of 30 years, from the 1940s to the 1970s. With the encouragement of their children, the dairy cows were sold in 1978 and they continued to farm the land.

Today the land owned by the Luther family is farmed by Matt and Brett Jennen.

Eleanor died in a tragic car accident in Otter Tail County in 1985. Leonard, with support of family and friends, continued to live on the farm he loved before passing away 25 years later.

District 96 classroom - 1954
Far left, front to back: Dick Luther, Dean Moore, Eileen Knudson,
David Moore, Perry Kugler, Joann Lunde
2nd row from left, front to back: Connie Lunde, Wayne Miller,
Nick Weyrens, Bill Luther, Mary Tomhave, Kathy Roehl
3rd row from left, front to back: Lois Luther, John Lunde,
unidentified girl, Earl Strande, Richard Tomhave
Far right, front to back: Bob Luther, Steve Roehl, Jim Lunde,
Keith Kugler, Jim Knudson, unidentified girl

Chapter Five

East Vernon, South Union

BOB LIEDL'S MEMORIES OF 516 EAST VERNON

Bob Liedl, FFHS Class of 1966, has great memories of his growing up years in Fergus Falls.

His parents, Max and Leetta, moved to 516 East Vernon Avenue before Bob was born.

A classmate of Liedl was Roger Bjorklund, who lived at 518 East Vernon. Roger's parents were Wally and Luella Bjorklund.

"Roger and I collected twine along a newly-paved road and wound it into a ball about two feet in diameter," Liedl recalled. "Roger used some for binding papers for his paper delivery job, and my mom used some in her large garden."

Liedl and Bjorklund, during their growing up years in Fergus Falls, also were close to classmate Steve Adelsman. His house contained his older brother's ham radio set.

"We would sit and listen to voices from around the world," said Liedl, retired and living in Neenah, Wisconsin, southwest of Green Bay, in 2020.

Bob Liedl, left, and Roger Bjorklund

As kids, Liedl and classmate Bruce Alstad trapped pocket gophers south of town and sold their feet. This was proof that the pocket gophers were killed.

"One time we went to check our traps and construction had begun on a roadway, so we lost all of the traps," Liedl said.

As they grew up, Liedl and Alstad did lots of fishing at Wall Lake, east of Fergus Falls, both summer and winter.

"I have lots of memories about standing on the sand bar off of Elks Point, driving in deep snow to get to the fish shanty, etc.," Liedl recalls.

Another favorite memory is playing kickball at Madison School (northwest corner of East Alcott and South Sheridan) with a tree as first base, the flagpole being second base and the corner of the building as third. A ball hit over the fence into the neighboring yard was a home run.

Liedl said that most people who grew up in Fergus Falls remember their first cars. His parents owned a 1947½ Hudson Hornet.

"There were half-year cars back then, not just the new model years which came out in October," notes Liedl.

"People used to name their cars. My high school girlfriend's was Myrtle, probably because the 1954 green Chevy resembled a turtle. My parents called theirs Betsy."

Liedl's first car was a 1955 Ford that he bought in 1965.

"I needed to get to work at Dave Steussy's (class of 1966) dad's Phillips 66 gas station on the west side of town. I later needed the car to get to work as a lifeguard at Pebble Lake."

He paid $125 for his Ford and sold it for $75 four years later.

"Lots of great times and memories with that car. I also remember the cars of others from our class, like Bob Neumann's 1965 white Oldsmobile convertible or Henry Rasmussen's cinnamon Chevelle SS396."

Another great car-related memory for Liedl and others is cruising from the Dairy Queen on East Vernon Avenue, driving along Washington Avenue downtown, cruising past

Skogmo's Café at the northwest corner of Mill Street and Lincoln Avenue downtown, heading north on Union Avenue to Dairyland, returning to East Vernon Avenue and heading south on Pebble Lake Road to the A&W Root Beer stand

"We'd then circle through A&W Root Beer and head back to the Dairy Queen, circle through that, and repeat, only occasionally, if ever, stopping for a soda. I was fortunate to live on Vernon Avenue at the time, and could sit out front and see many classmates drive by. Life was much simpler back then."

Liedl has many great memories of life guarding and teaching swimming lessons at Pebble Lake.

"This was a cold water lake. We watched the school buses come down the hill toward Pebble Lake, bringing kids while we worked for summer recreation director Oats LeGrand."

Several lifeguards, including Liedl, drove to Detroit Lakes to take lessons at an indoor pool and obtain certification as Water Safety Instructors (WSI).

"I still have Red Cross water safety books from those classes," Liedl said. "I laugh just reading with those illustrations."

Mary Rockwood was the head lifeguard and Chuck Brendecke, also with the Class of 1966, worked with Liedl as a lifeguard in the summers of 1964 and 1965.

"The chocolate Turtle® bars sold in the snack bar were the best, along with the frozen Snickers®," says Liedl.

He remembers kids on the south side of town ice skating during the winter months at Grotto Lake.

"I recall the old wooden-floor warming house where our mittens sizzled on the pot belly wood-burning stove," he says.

In the summer, Grotto Park had a great baseball diamond where neighbor kids played many games with as few or as many players as they could find. Grotto Park also was a great place to fly kites.

"Back then, the New York Yankees were THE team," Liedl says. "We all had our favorite major league players, such as Mickey Mantle with the Yankees, and we could name team lineups by heart."

He fondly remembers the old fairgrounds where Kennedy Secondary School now stands.

"We all looked forward to the county fair coming to town. Who could forget the 4-H barns, the midway with the rides and games of chance, the diggers, the ring toss, etc."

And while Liedl lived on East Vernon Avenue, his classmate Dave Sanderson lived on West Vernon Avenue.

"Dave and another classmate, Greg Peterson, were duck hunting buddies," Liedl said. "Many of our classmates also enjoyed fishing in the summer, ice fishing in the winter, riding bikes, deer hunting with our dads and being members of the Junior Rifle Club. We often had BB guns strapped to the side of our bikes. Yes, life really was much simpler back then."

BRUCE ALSTAD'S MEMORIES OF 708 SOUTH UNION

"I had many memories with Bob Liedl growing up," Bruce Alstad mentioned in June 2020. "We had a cottage near Elks Point on Wall Lake and did a lot of fishing on the lake."

Liedl and Alstad would ride their bikes with their fishing poles and BB guns from Fergus Falls to Wall Lake to fish and target practice.

He recalls the good life in Fergus Falls all four seasons of the year.

"It seemed like everyone we knew in our part of town did some ice skating on Grotto Lake and also at Lake Alice," Alstad said. "The pot belly stove at Lake Alice kept our feet warm and we appreciated the refreshment stand with hot chocolate."

He recalls a nice man at Lake Alice who was there to tend to the stove and tighten up the skates.

"A junk car was always put on the far end of Grotto Lake and it was a dollar bet to see when it would go through the ice, usually in March," Alstad recalls.

Many of the boys hunted ducks and pheasants with their dads and classmates during the 1950s and 1960s.

"We could practice with 22 rifles in the basement of Adams Elementary school and got the hunting safety license there," he says.

Alstad, in addition to hunting with Liedl, also has good memories of hunting with several other classmates, including Pat Osterberg, Don Balfour, Bruce Ritchey and Pat Sagerhorn.

Liedl and Alstad would also go fishing with Liedl's dad, Max, who would drive his big old Hudson to a lake to fish.

"I think Bob and I collected a 50 cents bounty on each pocket gopher we trapped," Alstad said. "The front feet were the evidence needed for the bounty."

Swimming lessons at Wall Lake were coordinated by the Red Cross.

Alstad also recalls the days at Washington Junior High.

"I signed Oats LeGrand's paddle for being 30 seconds late to gym class," he said.

Alstad was like most teenagers who had cars and drove around A&W restaurant, passing by the Dairy Queen, driving through downtown Fergus Falls and heading up north on Union Avenue to Dairyland.

"We did this over and over again," says Alstad.

MORE FROM BRUCE ALSTAD

"I remember playing marbles at recess. We would dig a hole in the dirt and try and put our cat's-eye marbles in the hole. We carried the marbles in a sock, or mom made a sack from the pocket from a pair of old pants in which we carried the marbles.

"At Bob Liedl's house, we drew a circle in the driveway and you had to knock out the marbles to win the cat's eyes. You were lucky if you had a big steely to use."

"Everyone had a pocket knife. I would cut a "Y" off a branch to make a slingshot. We got old rubber tubes from the bike shop in order to make the slingshot."

He remembers obtaining his hunter safety certificate while shooting .22s at targets in the basement of Adams School.

Some teachers and principals in the Fergus Falls school system could be very, very strict. Dick Richards and Alstad agreed that one of these stern people was the old principal at Adams School.

"My father was 100 percent Norwegian and made a sauna in our basement like most Scandinavians," he said. "I often used it to lose weight for wrestling at the high school."

"My Father had an airplane at the local airport and would take me flying around the area. He was also a certified mechanic to work on the planes at the airport. Dad and my uncle would shoot fox from the plane and land with skis to retrieve the fox for a bounty. I saw pictures of my father and uncle with a dozen gray and red fox."

He recalls one long family trip in the plane to Denver.

Alstad says that Fergus Falls was a great smaller community in which to live in Minnesota.

"My father started his business by fixing oil furnaces in Fergus Falls. He then went into selling and servicing dairy equipment with his brother. When his brother moved to Wisconsin they dissolved the business."

"He then started servicing industrial heating. My father would travel to South America, Europe and the Middle East to fix industrial heating. The last few years he was superintendent of heating systems on nuclear power plants being built."

"My mother got a job as a nurse, and I worked as a laborer for several years to pay for my college. She was a nurse in the Fergus Falls hospital, working in surgery and ER."

Alstad later on raised a family in Pennsylvania.

One sad note for Bruce was the death of his brother Doug, 8, from cancer in 1964 when Bruce was 16. He cherishes the photo in this chapter which includes Bruce, Doug and their cousin Roger.

"A very difficult time for my family," Bruce said.

*l-r: Bruce Alstad (16) his brother Doug (8),
and their cousin Roger in 1964*

Chapter Six

Carlisle School

HANS RONNEVIK'S CARLISLE MEMORIES

Long-time Fergus Falls residents and people who grew up in this area, especially during the 1950s and 1960s, recall driving through the town of Carlisle along old Highway 52 before the days of I-94.

This was the first town travelers went through when driving the 60 or so miles from Fergus Falls to Fargo-Moorhead. Other towns on the route were Rothsay, Lawndale, Barnesville, Baker and Sabin.

Hans Ronnevik, Fergus Falls High School Class of 1963, grew up on a farm near Carlisle along with his brothers Richard and Rolf and sisters Ruth and Mary. Their parents were Jorolf and Alice Ronnevik.

Long-time residents also remember the Carlisle General Store, post office, railway depot and grain elevator. Townspeople and Carlisle area farmers alike had the respect of Fergus Falls area residents for being hard-working people in Otter Tail County.

Carlisle area residents, like most inhabitants of the western part of the county, took pride in their Norwegian and Swedish ancestry. Carlisle Township was organized on February 24, 1881.

At one time, Otter Tail County had 289 rural schools, the most of any county in Minnesota.

CARLISLE COUNTRY SCHOOL RECOLLECTIONS

Hans Ronnevik has many grade school recollections from his eight years in Carlisle Country School District 286.

"I started out as a young five-year-old first grader in the fall of 1951, in the big brick schoolhouse that had all eight grades," Hans recalls. "My first teacher was Miss Delores Muth, and she was my teacher through third grade."

Then came Mrs. Jean Piechowski in fourth grade, Miss Alma Baumgartner in fifth and sixth grades, and Mrs. Harry Fretland for seventh and eighth grades.

There was no kindergarten in those days.

"The seventh and eighth graders really seemed big when we started out," Hans says, "and we looked up to them almost in awe."

After a couple of years there were too many students for the one-room school building. A second building, a white schoolhouse, was purchased by the school district and moved onto a lot just west of the original brick building.

"During the time when the basement and foundation were being put in place, I recall using the Carlisle Hall just across the road to the south for the lower four grades," Ronnevik says. "During recess we watched the construction

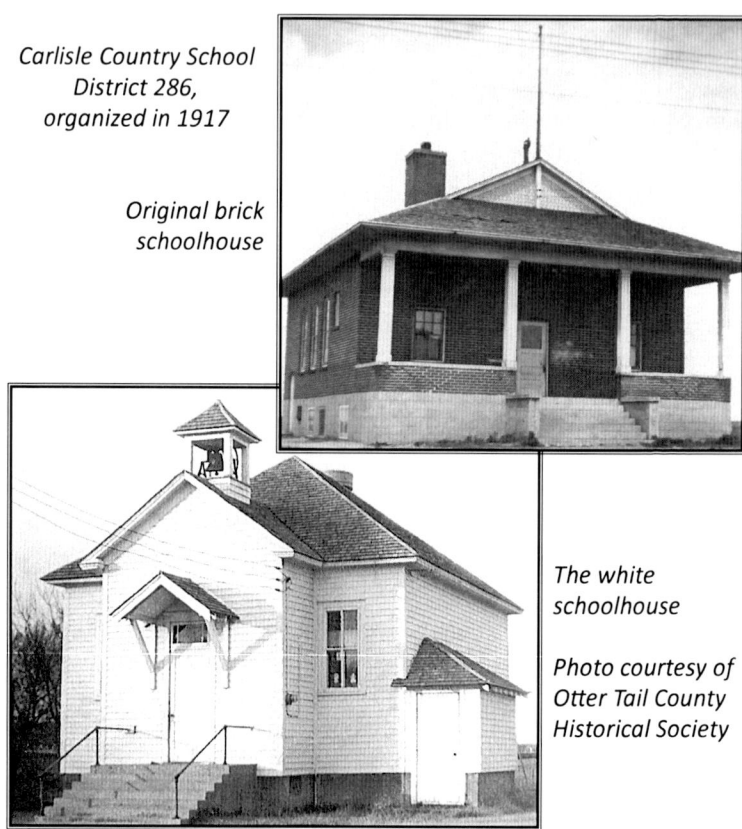

Carlisle Country School
District 286,
organized in 1917

Original brick
schoolhouse

The white
schoolhouse

Photo courtesy of
Otter Tail County
Historical Society

and saw the plumber melt lead ingots and use the molten lead to seal the joints in the new sewer lines."

He spent part of one year and at least one full year in the new white school building. It had a big bell tower with a bell operated by a rope to call students in to begin the school day, and back to the classroom from noon hour and recess time.

The new basement was a good place to play and do projects, which included woodworking when there was time off from classes or when students had specific industrial arts periods.

The big brick schoolhouse had no bell, other than the loud handbell that teachers rang every day.

"We started off each day with the Pledge of Allegiance to the Flag and often had singing that included patriotic songs," Hans recalled. "During the day we studied at our desks and were called up to a table at the front of the room for our individual class instruction in the various subjects. It was always fun to listen to the other classes if we had our work completed." He believes he and other students learned a lot by listening to the classes in the higher grades.

"Besides our individual class instruction, our teachers would often read books to the entire group. As we got older, we had important jobs: putting up the flag and taking it down at the end of the day, cleaning the blackboard, pounding the chalk dust from the erasers and burning the garbage."

For several years in the big school, Ronnevik and his classmates had no running water.

"We had smelly chemical toilets and had to carry in water for drinking. A couple of the older students would use a five-gallon shotgun pail and together carry water from the old stockyard pump, which was located by the railroad at the south edge of town."

"We lifted that full pail up over our heads and poured the water into a gravity-fed drinking fountain that worked almost

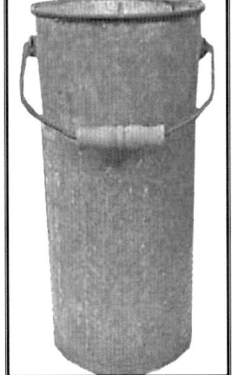

Shotgun pail

as well as the drinking fountains we have now."

He says that, likely, the big school got running water and updated plumbing when the white schoolhouse was brought in.

"We brought our own lunch buckets with sandwiches, cookies, fruit, milk, etc., for our noon lunch. During the winter we were able to have hot lunches."

Students had a basin filled with two to three inches of water that fit over a two-burner electric hotplate. Into it students set their glass jars containing food from home to be heated before they ate it.

"We loosened the lids so the jars would not crack when heated. Then we set the jars on top of a wire grill in the water bath to let our food warm up until it was time to eat. Usually, one student was in charge of this process."

"Most of the time it went well, but there were several ruined meals when a jar cracked and spilled the contents into the water."

At some point, pasteurized and homogenized milk cartons were delivered every day for a mid-morning milk break and for noon school lunches.

"That milk did not taste very good," Hans said, "for those of us used to unpasteurized milk fresh from our cows. When chocolate milk was made available for the morning milk break, it was a better-tasting option."

The white milk went down passably well with the noon meal.

A one-hour noon hour and a half-hour recess in the afternoon were always welcome times to play games or have organized physical education activity – maybe tumbling on big mats or a hard-played game of dodgeball.

"In cold weather we played games and spent recess in the basement, which had a wood floor and a bar to do chin-ups. When the weather was good in the spring and fall, our activity of choice was softball."

The country schools developed many good softball players who went on to play fast-pitch softball in 4-H, church and city leagues. After the country schools closed, those kinds of softball leagues went downhill.

That is when slow-pitch softball came in, and later fast-pitch softball ended up being a girls' high-school sport, while the boys ended up playing mostly baseball.

"In the spring of the year, we often were able to have our own field day competitions, with high jumping, broad jumping, softball throwing, three-legged wheelbarrow and sack racing, and the like. As far as I recall, we always ended with a softball game. Several times we hosted another country school, or they hosted us for our field day events."

Winter noon hours involved eating quickly and getting dressed into winter coats, snow pants and boots.

"Then we headed out on the five-minute walk to the Sethre Hill with our sleds for a time of sledding, skiing, and tobogganing. Sometimes we even carried pails of water to ice up a sledding run, which might even include a tunnel. When the first bell rang, it was time to quit and rush back in time to sweep the snow off from each other outside on the school porch."

Their wet clothes and mittens were stuffed into the big square holes of the large wall heat vent to be dried before they went home. Boots were set out to dry too, and students had to hurry to be ready for the second bell. That signaled their return to schoolwork and afternoon classes.

"During some of those years, a skating rink was flooded during the coldest months. After it froze solid, we could skate close by the school instead of going up to the Sethre Hill all the time."

Valentine's Day and Halloween were times to party.

"We exchanged valentines by putting those we brought into a big Valentine Box. During the afternoon party time, usually in the last hour of the school day, these were distributed. I remember having treats to eat and drink."

During Halloween, the students were usually dressed in costumes and often had pictures taken on the steps leading up to the pillared front porch in front of the big brick schoolhouse.

If students had birthdays during the school year, they often took a trip to the Carlisle Store and came back with big five-cent candy bars for everyone. Among the treats were Baby Ruth®, Mounds®, Hersheys®, Snickers® and the like.

Hans had his birthday during Christmas vacation, so he did not share treats like this during the school year.

Springtime was a time to clean up the school yard, including the big ball field just north of the brick schoolhouse. The ball diamond, with a big backstop behind it, faced the road north of the school yard and occasionally someone would hit a ball across the road.

"When the appointed cleanup day came, we all brought our gloves, rakes, maybe a spade and whatever else was needed for the job. We would line up with our rakes across the whole lawn. Soon we had long rows of dead grass, leaves and any garbage that was in our path to gather up in piles and burn on the road." When cleanup was finished, it signaled the beginning of the softball season in earnest.

"When it warmed up in the springtime, or maybe it was on warm fall days, I recall going on hikes to study nature for science classes. We would sometimes walk westward for a little less than a mile to Lake Oscar to collect shells, crayfish, vegetation and other items that we could study."

Other times they would walk north for a longer distance to some small lakes and sloughs on some Sethre land. Hans recalls being tired on the return trip, carrying specimens that might have included small jars of murky lake water full of living things to study the next day.

Other memorable events included taking a train trip, likely just for grades 5 through 8.

One classmate, Larry Johnson, recalled being so excited about this that he hardly slept a wink the night before. In the morning, the *Red River* passenger train made a special stop for Hans and his classmates at the Carlisle train depot and took them to Minneapolis.

"We then boarded a tour bus that took us to the State Capitol, Fort Snelling and the Ford Motor Company assembly plant, among other places of interest. I'm sure we had a lot to talk about on our train trip back to Carlisle later that day, and we were likely very tired."

There were also shorter trips like going to Fergus Falls and touring the museum in the county courthouse south of downtown Fergus Falls, the Coke Plant, and seeing the *Daily Journal* being assembled and printed.

"On one of these outings, we met singer Peggy Lee at some sort of event at the Fergus Falls Armory. I think there were day trips to the Fargo-Moorhead area as well. I seem to recall being at *WDAY-TV* and being on the *Party Line* show, maybe touring the *Fargo Forum*.

Just east of Moorhead, in Dilworth, Hans and his Carlisle classmates enjoyed seeing the old coal-fired and steam-powered train engine.

"Toward the end of the school year, we often had large county-wide music festivals in the new senior high gymnasium in Fergus Falls. That was always a fun time, singing together all the songs we had worked on during the past year."

Teachers from the various schools patrolled the group, keeping them in line and on task. There were many pea shooters confiscated during those events.

He also remembers going to downtown Fergus Falls during the noon break and looking at new softball gloves and bats, as well as checking out the five-and-ten-cent stores.

Christmas programs were always fun times. Students took time off from classwork to practice programs consisting of singing, plays, recitations, etc. Those programs were held in the Carlisle Hall with its raised stage and roll-up curtain with the picture of a cowboy on a horse, surrounded by advertisements from area businesses of that era.

That curtain is still in use in the new Carlisle Hall, built in the fall and winter of 1979-1980 with donated money and labor from throughout the Carlisle community.

The old hall had chair seating on the floor and bleachers in the back. The entire community turned out for those events. The evening Christmas program was topped off with a big gift exchange and the appearance of Santa Claus, who tromped up the stairs from the hall basement to the sounds of bells and "Ho, ho, ho-s."

Santa had brown bags filled with hard candies, cream-filled chocolates, and nuts. Some adults passed out oranges and/or apples from big boxes to everyone there. Then the students were off for Christmas vacation.

The school picnic at Long Lake at the end of the school year was another event that students looked forward to. They did a lot of visiting, enjoyed a big potluck, and participated in relay races for all ages and a softball game.

At the end of the day, there were ice cream treats scooped from big cardboard buckets purchased from Wee Villa Resort. Then it was goodbye as far as that year of school was concerned.

"But most of us still saw each other often at church, 4-H, and other community gatherings, as these were year-round activities," notes Hans.

His classmates during those years were Kay Sethre, Kathy Stenerson, Peter Loken, Owen Heiserman, and Larry Johnson.

"We had a great education in the country schools and went on to do well when we moved to other schools at the end of our eight years. In my case, and for all of us except Larry Johnson, that meant going to ninth grade in the old Fergus Falls Washington Junior High."

Hans' father, Jorolf Ronnevik, had attended Washington School when it was still the high school.

"Starting in sixth grade, Larry's family spent winters in Mesa, Arizona. Larry recalls that when he returned to Minnesota in the spring, he had to play catch up because the country school was farther along in our study material than his Arizona schools."

Larry attended high school in Arizona and in Rothsay, and graduated from Rothsay High School.

"Moving to junior high in Fergus Falls was quite a change for a farm boy like me," Hans says.

"Many of our Fergus Falls classmates had been together for several years by now, and we had to find our places among them in a class of more than 180 instead of only six. That happened quickly, and soon we felt part of those classes."

"Our country grade schools had prepared us well for the times ahead – high school and college and beyond."

District 286 graduating class of 1964 was the largest ever in the school's history. County Superintendent, Vernon Bachman, was there to hand out diplomas to the thirteen 8th-graders during the first-ever formal graduation ceremony held at the school.

Back, l to r: John Sethre, Steven Fjestad, Paul Heiserman, Mark Tysver and Richard (Ricky) Moen. Front, l-r: Noreen Skistad, Yvonne Stenerson, Arla Fjestad, Rebecca (Becky) Fjestad, Annette Hexum, Ruth Ronnevik, Barbara (Barb) Fjestad and Linda Eide.

Chapter Seven

Carlisle Store, Town Hall & Farmers Club

CARLISLE STORE WAS VILLAGE FOCAL POINT

Many area residents remember the years following World War II when the Carlisle Store was the center of activity in the small farming community just northwest of Fergus Falls.

Those were the days when drivers passed through Carlisle along the old Highway 52, prior to the construction of I-94.

The history of the store was chronicled by the late Jorolf Ronnevik, who farmed near Carlisle.

The store, which also housed the post office, was built for Chris and Mollie Evjen in 1916.

"This was the primary grocery store for area farm families," Ronnevik wrote. "There also were some hardware items sold, among them forks, hoes, nails, bolts and files."

Chris Evjen was also the railroad depot agent. The mail would arrive in Carlisle on the local train, then was carried to the post office. After school, children would run to the post office to get the family mail before heading home.

The Ronnevik family in 1972
front, l-r: Jorolf, Alice and Richard
back, l-r: Rolf, Ruth, Hans and Mary

Ronnevik, of Norwegian descent, farmed near Carlisle and lived on the family farm for 61 years. He was 103 when he died in 2019.

Speaking and reading Norwegian, along with translating many of his father's writings from Norwegian to English, were very important to him.

"Shopping was different in the early days of the Carlisle Store," Ronnevik said. "We would often hand our grocery list to the storekeeper, who then filled the order."

Jorolf remembered when, as a young man, his parents sent him to the Carlisle Store. He walked from the farm, carrying a few dozen eggs in a basket to exchange for some grocery items.

"Eggs, for most of the farmers, were the main source of grocery money," wrote Ronnevik. "When we needed kerosene for lamps and lanterns, the storekeeper took our can out to the shed behind the store to fill it from a barrel."

A gas pump was installed in front of the store.

"This was a hand-operated pump that pumped the gas into the 10-gallon glass tank at the top of the pump," said Ronnevik. "Then the gas would flow by gravity through a hose into the parked auto."

The tank was marked with one-gallon increments, so it was easy to see exactly how much was sold.

"Over the years, the post office in Carlisle added to the incomes of the storekeepers," noted Ronnevik. "The storekeeper was also the postmaster or postmistress. This also brought the post office boxholders to the store, which helped business."

Carlisle Store business was good into the 1950s, but changes were taking place. Kerosene was no longer needed, and a nearby filling station took over the gas business in Carlisle.

In 1960, Oliver Teterud took over ownership of the store and ran it until 1973. That year the final owners became Art and Jeanette Amundson.

Chain stores in nearby Fergus Falls lured more and more customers from Carlisle. The final blow came with the closing of the Carlisle post office.

The Amundsons closed their business in 1983. They sold the building to Dennis and Dorothy Madsen, who transformed the structure into a house.

The Carlisle Store, however, was never forgotten.

THE CARLISLE HALL AND FARMERS CLUB

Jorolf Ronnevik recalled that on a site about 50 yards east of the present town hall stood another Carlisle Hall that for many years was the center of the community. This was a concrete building constructed in the early 1920s from blocks made in nearby Elizabeth.

It was in the old building where the Carlisle Band gave concerts, meetings for Carlisle 4-H took place, and where the Carlisle Farmers Club gathered.

The Farmers Club was a forum for debates and speeches. Speakers included political candidates, attorneys, school administrators, county agents, businessmen and pastors.

On Farmers Club night, Henry Haldorson, the de facto mayor of Carlisle, would turn on the street lights and people would come, filling the hall.

"I remember that in the early 1920s they would come in their Model T Fords, their Chevrolets and Buicks, Dodges, Dorts and other cars," Ronnevik wrote. "In winter, if the roads were plugged, they came on foot or with horse teams and sleds."

He said that the teams were put inside the shelter at the stockyards until it was time to go home.

"Only a blinding snowstorm would cause a cancellation of Farmers Club night," Jorolf recalled, "and then it would be rescheduled as soon as possible."

The meetings always opened after the curtain was raised. There were a few musical selections by the Carlisle Trio, with Petrina Fjestad on the piano, Oscar Lien playing violin and Ted Fjestad on the cello.

"Then the club president, Peter Fjestad, a man of dignity with always the right words, would come on stage," Ronnevik recalled.

Fjestad praised the Carlisle Trio and then opened the business portion of the meeting with announcements.

Music was a big part of every meeting. Later on the Trio became the Carlisle Orchestra, with family members joining the group. Philip Fjestad became pianist, replacing his mother, Petrina.

There also were archery demonstrations, and others performed magic tricks. Charles Beck of Fergus Falls demonstrated the art of painting.

The age of television led to the demise of the Farmers Club. Improved automobiles made it easier to go elsewhere for entertainment.

The old hall lives on. That's because the new hall, built in 1979, has maple flooring that came from the old hall, as well as the roll-up stage curtain. Advertising blocks on the curtain surround a large central picture of a cowboy on a horse.

Chapter Eight

East Lakeside Drive

PETE ELLINGSON'S MEMORIES

Pete Ellingson, a 1965 graduate of Fergus Falls High school, says that Judge Roger Dell lived a few doors south of his family on East Lakeside Drive, near Lake Alice.

Pete Ellingson

"We would play basketball at Dr. Lee's house next to the Dell house," Pete recalled. "Judge Dell would always say 'Hi,' and wanted to shoot at least one shot of the basketball before getting into his big car."

The Dell house was also very big for just the two of them, Ellingson said.

"My Dad, Edson Ellingson, knew Judge Dell quite well, and so did Claude Reitan, my godfather. They were all near the same age and did many business dealings around the area."

Pete's father was the manager of the local office of the Federal Land Bank for 35 years and retired in 1967. The office was located south of Otter Tail Power Company on Washington Avenue and was a nice hangout for Pete to work on the old adding machine.

Edson Ellingson was also on the city water commission for many years.

"I remember going up to see the new water plant on the hill by Hoot Lake as a kid, and I also had many visits to the City Hall for meetings," Pete says.

His mother, Nora, was a substitute teacher at Lincoln, Cleveland and Jefferson schools when Pete and his brother, Tom, were in their junior and senior high school days.

Pete would always use Lake Alice for fun during both warm and cold weather.

"The winters and the Winter Wonderland bonfires were always a big hit at the southeast corner of the lake," he says. "The city would toss just about everything in the pile but the kitchen sink, to make the fire burn big."

He says that time of the year held a special place in the hearts of all residents with all the Winter Wonderland events going on during the week, including the big talent show at Roosevelt Park Gymnasium, adjacent to the old high school.

The Black Knights rode around during Winter Wonderland with their charcoal pens. "They marked many a cheek back then. It was fun for some, but not for others," Pete recalled.

For some crazy winter fun, he and his friends would set up a big sail with an old bed sheet and a long pole, then head down to the frozen Lake Alice with ice skates in hand.

"If the ice was new and had no major snow piles or big expansion cracks, we were on our way at a very high rate of fun speed," he said.

In the summer, the city would put out the clipped-wing ducks for one and all to see swimming in the lake. Fergus Falls residents were told the clipped wings would not allow them to fly. City employees would then capture them in the fall with some big netting, and then it was off to the fairgrounds for winter storage.

Later on the geese took over the area and made a mess out of the islands and lakeside.

"My dad made an issue of going to City Hall to try to fix that, to no avail," Pete says. "I also remember, in the winter, they hauled tons of rock and other debris out to the center of Lake Alice to make a second island."

The first island is close to shore on the northeast side of the lake, where generations have fed the ducks and geese.

"Truckload after truckload, over a few winters, was hauled in to finally complete the additional island in the middle of the lake that everyone sees today," he said.

Pete says nobody really dared swim in the lake, as it had a very muddy bottom and was considered unsafe. Also, there was the belief that debris filled the lake following the 1919 tornado.

As a kid growing up in Fergus Falls, Ellingson admired his grade school physical education teacher, Fran Conito, who also served as Athletic Park coordinator.

"Fran always wanted to make sure we had the right size football helmets, shoes and suits," he said. "He was a big talker and very friendly guy."

One time in 6th grade Pete intercepted a pass while playing defensive end for his Cleveland grade school team.

Ice skating on the southwest side of Lake Alice
has been passed along from one generation to the next.

"Fran cheered more than anyone after I ran it back for a TD," Pete said.

"That was the kind of man he was, always patting you on the back and saying 'that a boy,' and that was really appreciated by us kids."

Ellingson has fond memories of the old fairgrounds at a site now occupied by Kennedy Secondary School in Fergus Falls.

"The local car dealers would store their new cars in the big activity building at the old fairgrounds, atop the hill that was across the street from the armory," he recalls.

"The new cars were covered up while coming into town, and then were brought over to that big building to store them before they were put into the showrooms each fall."

"My dad knew Norm Johnson of Minnesota Motor sales fame, and he would always take us to see the new cars under wraps at the fairgrounds."

Pete says, "It was quite a thrill to look under the covers and see the new car models, all big, long, two tones, with new gadgets and more. I think Norm did this for more than one person, as an old sales technique, I would imagine."

Norm, as any good salesman would, sold Pete his first new car, a Chevrolet Nova SS, after he returned home from the Army in January 1970.

His father, Edson, would always buy a new car every four years, mostly for business, as he had to drive around to the many farms in the Fergus Falls area for work.

"The fairgrounds, because it was so close to us, is also one giant memory. I remember falling asleep many a summer night listening to the sounds of the calliope (mechanical musical keyboard) of the Merry Go Round and more through our open second-story bedroom window."

He said the stock car races, held near the fairgrounds, were noisy, but were enjoyed immensely by spectators. Each had speed and crazy crashes.

The fairgrounds midway was mostly set up by Thomas Brothers Shows. The arcade-style games were run by a local company, Townsend Amusements.

"It was a real thrill to go on the Tilt-A-Whirl, the airplanes and more," Pete said. There were many buildings on the grounds and it was always a treat to see all the animals and local displays by many of the artisans of the time.

"More than once, we snuck in the tricky way, just to see if we could actually do it. There was a favorite route for that each year via the race track fences."

He says Norm Johnson "was quite the guy," and always had a great story or two to tell if a person ever stopped at the old Minnesota Motor location in downtown Fergus Falls, on South Court Street.

"I also remember many Minnesota Motor employees, including mechanic and classmate Warren Bjorklund's dad, Wally Bjorklund. He was also a city volunteer fireman."

When the siren went off, Bjorklund and other employees dashed over to the fire hall, at City Hall, just south of the Otter Tail River.

"It was always quite a thrill to watch the fire trucks leave the fire station and head down the street," Pete said. "I became a volunteer fireman myself because of those great memories of seeing that and visiting City Hall while in Boy Scouts."

Pete fondly recalls going to all the other car dealers' showrooms back then, to check out the new cars each fall and beyond.

Another favorite person for Pete was Dutz Domholt, a former neighbor and salesman at the Ford dealership on West Lincoln Avenue across the street from what now is Service Food Market.

"Dutz always had a great story or two to tell us, of just about everything out there besides the cars he sold."

Many times, after Tuesday school, Pete would go over to check out the Nash Rambler dealer near his church, Bethlehem, and talk to the owner, Iram Worner. His son, Gerry, was a good neighborhood friend and Lincoln school classmate of Pete.

They had many play cars, trucks and train days at the Worner house on the west side of Lake Alice, more than one can remember.

Pete also checked out the Dodge dealer near the fire hall as Walt Skogmo, an Otter Tail Lake neighbor of the Ellingsons during the summer months, worked there and enjoyed showing all the cars, too.

After high school, Ellingson attended Fergus Falls Community College (now M State) and worked at Olson Furniture and Olson Funeral Home.

According to Pete, "It was a really fun time working there with the Olson crew. Bob, the owner, was a terrific leader of the troops and ran a tight ship and, I believe, is the reason they have survived to this day."

Pete says Bob's wife, Elaine, was a great help in keeping things in great order as well.

"Classmate Tom Kavanaugh and I always enjoyed making deliveries, laying carpet for Olson Furniture, and running errands for the funeral home. Bob's dad, Guy, was always around helping out with the many things a store needed, long after his retirement."

Bob's son, Guy, was named after his grandfather.

Pete also remembers the cool Townsend Record Shop on West Lincoln Avenue, where a kid could try out the record before buying it in the little booths inside the store. His older sister, Mary, would take him there in the late 1950s, since Pete was too young to do this on his own at the time.

"They (Townsend Record Shop) also supplied the music for the skating rink on Lake Alice. That was a real treat for us kid skaters, chasing the girls around the very big rink with the great music of our times blaring."

Looking back, Ellingson is amazed that Fergus Falls had seven public grade schools during his growing up years: Lincoln, Washington (which closed once Cleveland was built) Madison, Jefferson, Eisenhower, McKinley and Adams. He attended two of them and enjoyed his times there immensely. He still enjoys seeing old friends made back then.

LAKE ALICE GROCERY HOLDS SPECIAL MEMORIES

One last great memory, says Pete, "is all the time we spent at Charlie's corner grocery store near the southeast side of Lake Alice."

Pete and other neighborhood kids all enjoyed stopping at this grocery store, named Lake Alice Grocery, to have a Coke®, Nesbitt® Orange Soda, Hires® Root Beer, Hershey® Bar, Salted NutRoll and more.

Many Fergus Falls High School grads remember walking up the hill from the old high school along Friberg Avenue, during the noon hour to purchase candy at Lake Alice Grocery. The owners were Charlie and Inga Johnson.

"I lived close by, on the southeast side of the lake, so I was in Lake Alice Grocery almost every day," said Margaret Larson, FFHS Class of 1966.

She later worked with refugee and immigrant populations as a clinical social worker in an outpatient clinic at the University of Minnesota's Academic Health Center.

Gert Larson, mother of Margaret Larson, who in 2021 still lived in her own home on the southeast side of Lake Alice, turned 105 in 2021 on Easter Sunday. Margaret was home from the Twin Cities for her mother's big celebration Easter weekend.

Lake Alice Grocery was located on the southeast side of Lake Alice.

A sign on her front yard stated, "Help Gert celebrate 105 years with a toot and a wave." She waved from inside her front window to many people passing by on foot or in cars.

Mary Melby Christenson, also in the Class of 1966, lived in that neighborhood until second grade. "We gave Gert a toot of the horn as my 97-year-old mother and I took a drive on Easter weekend," said Christenson.

Ann Johnson Arnold, FFHS Class of 1957, also has special memories. "We moved a few times when I was growing up in Fergus, and I mostly remember Lake Alice Grocery on the southeast side of the lake."

She also stayed close to Gert Larson over the years.

"Gert called me here in Oregon last year, in 2020, after she heard about my brother Myron's passing," said Ann. "We had a nice conversation for a half hour or so. She's amazing. I have her birthday date on my calendar."

The Ellingson house on East Lakeside Drive, Lake Alice

Chapter Nine

West Cavour, West Lincoln

WEST CAVOUR, WEST LINCOLN MEMORIES

During the 1950s, the 900 and 1000 blocks of West Cavour Avenue were near the extreme west edge of Fergus Falls, long before the development of Fleet Farm and businesses close to what's now I-94.

The Hintgen family of me, parents Roy and Claire Hintgen, and my sisters Catherine and Mary lived at 930 West Cavour.

Some other West Cavour residents, and their addresses, are listed at the end of this chapter.

Nearby at the northwest corner of West Lincoln Avenue and Second Avenue stood Alice's Grocery, where kids purchased nickel candy bars and nickel bottles of seven-ounce pop.

Kids like me often biked over to purchase baseball cards, hoping to open a pack of cards and see if we were lucky enough to find a Mickey Mantle, Willie Mays, Ted Williams or Hank Aaron card. Alice's Grocery also was a favorite for my sisters, Catherine and Mary.

Hintgen family kids, about 1950, Catherine (top), Mary and Tom,
at 930 West Cavour Avenue on the north side of the street

Back then three tall towers with lights were close to what was then KGDE Radio Station, at what now is the northeast section of Fleet Farm. Across the street, which was the old Highway 210, were business establishments in what was referred to as Edgetown.

Included in Edgetown were a cabinet shop, Edgetown Lumber, livestock auction sales barn and International Harvester (farm equipment).

Kids used to hunt pheasants at a slough at what later became Fergus Falls Community College.

Those on the 900 and 1000 blocks of West Cavour oftentimes had deer, pheasants, and even stray cows in their back yards.

Ed Darby lived there for four years second through fifth grades. The Darby family later moved from West Cavour to the south side of town, east of Lake Region Hospital.

He has two vivid memories of West Cavour, and Mike and Paul Sigelman were a big part of this.

"Paul Sigelman was a very close friend, since we were the same age," says Ed, a 1960 graduate of Fergus Falls High School.

"In their back yard, Mike and Paul built a large two-tower snow fort, with the towers connected by a tunnel. Hours of fun."

The Sigelman brothers also collaborated to build a snow ramp, about three feet high, next to the street curb between the Roy Hintgen and Sam Sigelman properties. That ramp allowed kids to gather significant sled speed when accessing Cavour.

Darby said the relationship between the Sam Sigelman, Roy Hintgen, Dr. W.O.B. Nelson, Dick Raiter and Don Darby families was special.

"Each of the five men had a wonderful and creative sense of humor. We quickly learned to anticipate unexpected exploits 365 days a year."

Darby recalls nearby banker Louis Peavey's back yard as very large and open, allowing kids to play touch football.

"It was when residing on West Cavour when I made friends with Larry Dorn, who lived on Cavour approximately five blocks east of our home," Darby says. "Our relationship, after 71 years, remains strong and active."

Further west, almost to the end of Cavour Avenue, was an older kid, possibly by the name of Schultz, who was a very fine athlete. "He moved to Alexandria and captained the football team," notes Darby. "He would have graduated from high school about 1958."

Darby recalled these memories in 2020, as a retiree living in Fort Collins, Colorado.

JAN PRATT NELSON

Jan Pratt Nelson, who grew up at 1029 West Cavour Avenue, graduated from Fergus Falls High School in 1958. Today the home in which she lived is a short distance from the county museum, which was constructed in the early 1970s at Van Dyk Park.

"I remember hopscotch, kool aid stands, Ante-I-Over throwing the ball over the roof, seeing dads and kids in the neighborhood polishing cars on Saturday mornings, shooting basketball at places like the Jack West family home, seeing deer and pheasants in the back yard before the city of Fergus Falls moved westward, and friendships with Lynn, Steve and Charley Johnson."

Charley Johnson later became a TV anchor in Fargo, and after that headed the Fargo-Moorhead Convention and Visitors Center.

"While car pooling with Charlie West to school, we paid Charlie 50 cents a week for gas for our rides to school, even coming home for lunch."

"There was trick or treating at the home of Mr. Peavey, the banker, who made kids sign their names for a shot glass of jelly beans. He lived next to Wests."

"The winter fort we had in the slough where the county museum now stands was great fun. It was a wonderful place for hide and seek. Weeds were so tall and the slough was frozen."

"Cruising in town in Sam Sigelman's Chrysler, driven by sons Michael and Paul, was special fun."

JAN AT ALICE'S GROCERY

Jan Pratt Nelson, FFHS Class of 1958, was 15 when she started work for Alice's Grocery at the northwest corner of West Lincoln Avenue and Second Avenue, a block east of what today is the county museum. Jan said the grocery store owner, Alice Malmstrom, was a friend to everyone.

"Kids coming into the store with pennies to purchase candy were treated with respect, just as much as regular customers buying milk, bread, meat and other items."

Jan said the coffee pot was always on, and mailmen would take a break along their routes and stop at Alice's Grocery for a cup of coffee. Their coffee mugs had their names attached, and Alice kept those coffee mugs right at the grocery store."

"Sundays were especially busy, since the major grocery stores closed at 6 p.m. Saturday and didn't open again until Monday morning. That's when the corner grocery stores made most of their money," Jan recalls.

Alice's Grocery store at 902 West Lincoln Avenue was a favorite place for kids growing up on West Lincoln and also West Cavour. The building stood through the 1970s and was replaced by a business office.

KAREN KIELMEYER AT ALICE'S GROCERY

Karen Kielmeyer Matteson, FFHS Class of 1960, said she had her first real job, aside from babysitting, at Alice's Grocery on West Lincoln Avenue.

"I grew up on nearby Stanton Avenue. When working for Alice Malmstrom at the grocery store, I came to know a lot of people in the neighborhood. They'd charge for groceries. We'd write the order by hand in their charge book. Back then we used an old-fashioned, pull-handle cash register to handle money."

She recalled selling a lot of ice cream cones, Popsicles® and penny candy. During the 1950s, a penny or nickel went a long way when it came to purchases.

In 1958, Alice Olson asked Karen to work at Woolworth's in downtown Fergus Falls. Her first job was as a Easter bunny. "I dressed in a bunny outfit and handed out candy to the kids," she said. "I then graduated to become a regular Woolworth's clerk and worked in all departments."

"During summer Crazy Days, Woolworth's moved a freezer outside near Lincoln Avenue and filled it with ice cream sandwiches. We sold them for the crazy price of nine cents each."

Karen and her husband, Jack, lived in Sarasota, Florida, for more than 35 years. Karen worked for a bank, pursued a career in sales and did a lot of volunteer work over the years. Jack worked in government securities.

Jack and Karen have passed on, but their memories are still cherished.

JIM WEST, 920 WEST CAVOUR

Jim West, FFHS Class of 1962, remembers doing some work for Alice Malmstrom at Alice's Grocery Store on West Lincoln Avenue. "As a kid I used to mow her lawn, including the lot next to the store, and shovel her sidewalk and drive. She also had a large garden behind the store, down to the alley."

Jim remembers Anton "grandpa" Aas, who lived next door to the West family, as the custodian at McKinley Elementary School.

"We kids would try to keep up with him walking from school to home, but he was an Abe Lincoln type, with long legs," Jim recalls.

Speaking of coming home from school, one of the West dachshunds would sleep in the sun coming through the double windows in the master bedroom upstairs, but she would come down to the front door to greet Jim and his brothers every day. "She could not see or hear us coming."

There were some play accidents. One involved a neighbor, Mary Hintgen.

"We were playing some sort of ball game in the Hintgen back yard, and somehow I accidentally hit her in the mouth with the ball," Jim recalls. "Years later, Mary (who had perfect teeth) had the one tooth that got hit in front that was gray."

Another accident involved Jim.

"We were playing in the sprinkler in our back yard and throwing water at each other, but there were no plastic bottles back then, so we used glass. My glass bottle got hit and broke, leaving me with deep cuts on the palm of my right hand."

He remembers the housekeeper for Peaveys, who lived next door, bringing out the oriental rugs from their living room and dining room and unrolling them on the front lawn. They were blue oriental rugs and she would dye the worn areas to blend them in to the background of the rugs.

In the lot on Summit Avenue, to the north behind the Noyes' house, there were large slabs of granite stacked randomly across the back of the lot, believed to be left over from a bank under construction downtown. This became a neighborhood playground.

"Little did we know how unsafe they were," Jim says.

Speaking of Noyes, when Jim's father, Jack West, was looking for a house in 1944, the one house that was for sale was the Noyes house. But it was short one bedroom and Frank Noyes suggested that Jack buy his house at 920 West Cavour. The Noyes family move two doors to the west.

Jim also remembers a red four-wheel bike that all three of the boys would use. It had disappeared by the time younger brother Pete came along.

John West on his four-wheeler at 920 West Cavour

A couple of years before moving from Fargo to Fergus Falls, Jim's mother Charlotte won a green Pontiac, plus 1,000 gallons of Texaco gas, from Ivory Snow®.

"Dad added what we called the 'too-taw' (that is what it sounded like) horn to it, and it was used to call us home for dinner. Its distinctive sound could be heard for blocks."

When the car was traded in, Jack West mounted the horn inside the garage and added a doorbell switch in the front hall, so Charlotte could still use it to call her boys home for dinner.

"A couple of things Dad did to 920 West Cavour, when we first moved in, was to weather strip all the doors and windows, and strip the mahogany-colored stain from the oak floors and finish them a natural oak color. This must have been fun with two boys and an infant living there."

LYNN TOMHAVE MERRITT

"It was a fun time for all of us growing up on West Cavour Avenue," said Lynn Tomhave Merritt, who in 2021 resided in Elbow Lake.

The Tomhave address was 1009 West Cavour. Pearl Greenwood resided on one side of their home, to the east, and Harold and Ginger Devries were on the other side, to the west.

Lynn's parents were Ella Tomhave, a stay-at-home mom in those days, and Dean Tomhave, the owner of General Trading Co., an auto parts store on Washington Avenue.

Lynn's sister Jeanne (Loken), was a teacher and is married to Peter Loken of Carlisle, northwest of Fergus Falls.

"I have many memories growing up on West Cavour, a perfect childhood neighborhood," said Lynn, a 1967 graduate of Fergus Falls High School. "Neighbor Vicki Pratt and I played together most days."

On one particular day, they decided to cross the street from the Pratt house to an area that today is the county museum. "We decided to make mud pies, but before we knew it, we were both stuck in the mud and losing our shoes. Luckily, Vicki's big brother, Kendall, saw that we were in trouble."

"Kendall put on some high boots and pulled each one of us out. He carried us to their house. Florence, Vicki's mom, was not very happy with us. She put us both in the bathtub before she sent me home."

During a particular school day, when kids on West Cavour woke up, they saw that the rain had frozen everywhere, including on the roads and sidewalks.

"Stephi Araskog, Vicki Pratt and I decided to skate to school," Lynn recalls. "We made it to McKinley school and were greeted by Miss Chelgren, the principal. She told us that was not a good idea."

In the summer, after all the neighborhood dads were through with work for the day, one of the dads would decide to play horseshoes.

"We had a horseshoe pit in our back yard," Lynn recalls. "One dad would start clanging the shoes, calling the men in the neighborhood to play. The moms also got the message and prepared a pot luck dish to pass around."

When the men finished their games of horseshoe, everyone would have a wonderful time visiting and eating a delicious meal.

MARTY RAITER FRAMPTON'S MEMORIES

"All the memories on West Cavour were wonderful for me," Marty says. "Mary Hintgen and I were best friends. It was also fun to play with her older sister, Catherine."

Marty remembers Catherine Hintgen falling out of a tree in the back yard of the Raiter house and breaking her arm. "That was scary for me and my family."

Marty remembers the pipe organ that Roy Hintgen used to play in the basement.

"I remember watching many TV shows at the Hintgen house. The TV show *Dragnet* was one that scared me, so I had to go home when that came on."

Marty and her family later moved to Colorado, but have returned to this area in the summers to stay at Otter Tail Lake.

SOME WEST CAVOUR RESIDENTS

907 – Irvin and Marie Anderson: Irvin operated Andy's 66 Service.

913 – Julia Hauberg: Julia was the owner of Hauberg Jewelry.

920 – Jack and Charlotte West: Jack was an attorney for Otter Tail Power and headed Junior Rifle Club.

923 – Llyal and Mildred Hanson: Lyal worked in county government; Mildred (Micky) was a special education teacher.

924 – Louis and Maude Peavey: Louis was president of Fergus Falls National Bank.

927 – Dr. W.O.B. Nelson and Dagney.

927 – Warren and Marion Araskog (after Nelsons moved away): Warren worked for Victor Lundeen & Company.

928 – Gordy and Mary Fran Ebersviller: Gordy was co-owner of Ebersviller Implement.

930 – Roy and Claire Hintgen: Roy was co-owner of Hintgen-Karst Electric Company.

934 – Sam and Marilyn Sigelman: Sam owned Sigelman Hide & Fir.

934 – Fred and Cele Heisel (later owners): Fred worked for the state health department; Cele was a junior high Latin teacher.

937 – Don and Dorothy Darby: Don owned Darby Travel and Insurance Agency.

940 – A.T. and Hazel Van Dyk: A.T. was park superintendent for the city of Fergus Falls; Hazel taught piano lessons.

1005 – Pearl Greenwood: Pearl was co-owner of City Café & Bakery.

1019 – Dean and Ella Tomhave: Dean owned General Trading Co., an auto parts store.

1020 – LeRoy and Joan Anderson: LeRoy was a policeman for the city of Fergus Falls.

1029 – Bob and Florence Pratt: Bob worked for National Tea Packing Plant.

1026 – Vern and Irene Johnson: Vern was a salesman for a pharmaceutical company.

1027 – Jim and Florence Renner: Jim worked for Northwestern Bell Telephone.

1032 – Ed and Marguerite Belka: Ed worked for Edgetown Lumber Company.

The swing set in the back yard of the Hintgen house, late 1940s and early 1950s, was a popular place for neighbor kids as well.

Chapter Ten

Van Dyk House

MEMORIES OF THE VAN DYK HOUSE

Many long-time residents, and others who call Fergus Falls their hometown, recall the days in the 1940s, 1950s and 1960s of being dropped off at 940 West Cavour Avenue. It was there where they took piano lessons from the legendary Hazel Van Dyk.

This was, and still is, a stately Victorian house in a park-like setting positioned further back than other nearby houses on the north side of West Cavour Avenue.

Hazel not only gave piano lessons at their home, but also held piano recitals at their large residence.

Today the house, on the west side of Fergus Falls, is a half block east of what today is the county museum.

Hazel's husband, Anthony (A.T.) Van Dyk, was a native of Holland who served as park superintendent in Fergus Falls. His joy, in addition to tending to his expansive flower garden near his house, was supervising the planting of trees and beautiful flowers at city parks throughout Fergus Falls.

A.T. and Hazel Van Dyk resided in this house at 940 West Cavour Avenue, Fergus Falls, from the 1940s to the 1960s. A.T. was city park superintendent and Hazel was a renowned piano instructor.

The new owners of this classic home are Krehl and Meghan Stringer, who moved to Fergus Falls from Bemidji in July 2020. Pastor Krehl had received a call as chaplain at PioneerCare retirement community.

Meghan has been a piano and voice teacher for more than 20 years.

"I was amazed at the coincidence that I shared the same occupation with Hazel," she said. "It must have been a sign that this house was meant for us."

Krehl and Meghan say they were attracted to the home's grandeur, history and immaculate preservation.

"When we toured the house, we were taken with the high ceilings and beveled glass windows in the dining and living rooms," Meghan said. "We notice, with the sunrise, that the beveled glass acts as a prism and we see many little rainbows reflected on walls opposite the windows."

She says the cranberry stained-glass window upstairs is unique and beautiful. At sunset, pink is reflected off everything in the path of the sunlight from that window.

They say the carpentry and woodwork throughout the house is stately.

"We have a beautiful staircase with carved support columns," Meghan said.

Krehl notes that there are eight-inch baseboards throughout the house, huge pocket doors, hardwood floors, and beautiful wood doors with the original doorknobs.

"On a practical level," says Meghan, "we needed a home large enough to accommodate the antiques we have inherited and collected. People have commented that the inside of the house looks like a museum."

Krehl and Meghan had enjoyed having two acres of land in Bemidji, so they wanted a large lot in Fergus Falls. The half-acre was just right – not too much work, but at the same time affording them the opportunity to enjoy the outdoors.

The property on West Cavour Avenue is indeed park-like, with the number and variety of trees and beautiful gardens.

"We noticed the other homes in the neighborhood were well maintained," Meghan said. "We have since enjoyed getting to know our friendly neighbors."

Shortly after moving here, Meghan visited the Otter Tail County Historical Society's museum a half block to the west. She picked up a book, *Building from the Past*, written by James Gray and Marjorie Barton and published by the Fergus Falls Heritage Preservation Commission. Page 107 describes their house.

They now have the abstracts of prior owners of the property. The oldest abstract dates from 1871. A.T. and Hazel Van Dyk appear as "grantors" on the mortgage deed from March 25, 1940. The Van Dyk name continues on the abstracts until 1966, when A.T. Van Dyk passed away.

Former piano students of Hazel Van Dyk recall the days of the 1940s, 1950s and 1960s taking piano lessons in that stately house.

One of them is Janet Preus, a 1967 graduate of Fergus Falls High School.

"I'll never forget Hazel encouraging me and saying, rhythmically, 'Sink to the bottom of the keys.' She was an excellent piano teacher."

Charley Johnson lived four houses to the west of the Van Dyk house; he took piano lessons from Hazel for three years. He later became a TV news anchor in Fargo.

MEMORIES FROM ANN JOHNSON ARNOLD

"My first piano lessons were from Hazel Van Dyk in her home on West Cavour Avenue. I remember the grand piano was in the dining room for lessons and recitals," says 1957 Fergus Falls High School graduate Ann Johnson Arnold.

She still has several marked-up piano lesson books.

The first book, *Stunts: a very first exercise book*, shows Hazel's penciled notes throughout the pages with blue and red stars applied next to some of the titles.

"I remember being quite nervous during recitals while playing for an audience of mostly parents sitting in the living room," Arnold says. "Hazel prepared the special recital programs using a typewriter, some original and some carbon copies, listing the students' names and their piano pieces."

Because of space, each recital was limited to about six to ten students. One recital program listed nine boys, including Arnold's brother Myron Johnson, along with Richard Baker and Jack Mouritsen.

Myron Johnson and Richard Baker were in the FFHS Class of 1956 and Mouritsen was in the FFHS Class of 1957.

MEMORIES FROM MARILYN SAURE BRECKENRIDGE

"Piano lessons with Mrs. Van Dyk were an important part of my growing up in Fergus Falls," says Marilyn Saure Breckenridge, FFHS Class of 1957. "Every Thursday I had a piano lesson during the school year, and every day except Sundays were practice days."

In order to get out of doing dishes, she would often say she needed to practice on the piano.

Saure-Breckenridge grew up in a family where the two priorities were music and church.

"My older sister Mabeth Saure had a beautiful singing voice. She started singing solos at age three, and started piano lessons with Mrs. Van Dyk at age four. Mabeth was a born musician and I think she was one of Mrs. Van Dyk's favorite students."

Mabeth won one contest after another and ended up playing in the Ten Piano Concert at Northrup Auditorium at the University of Minnesota in Minneapolis. Marilyn was proud to be her sister.

Adds Marilyn, "Mrs. Van Dyk never entered me to play in any competition, but I reached a level to be able to play hymns, which served me well in planning worship services as an ordained pastor in the Lutheran Church."

She would always say that the spoken word spoke to the mind, while music spoke to the heart.

"I also find now in retirement I often sit down at our piano and play hymns and the pieces I learned when I was a student of Mrs. Van Dyk. My cherished piano book was a Chopin book that has Mrs. Van Dyk's written notations in it."

Her favorite piece that she learned to play and memorize in that book was *Polonaise in A Major.*

"Mrs. Van Dyk taught me not only to play the piano but to enjoy listening to music. It has been said that the only proof needed for the existence of God is music."

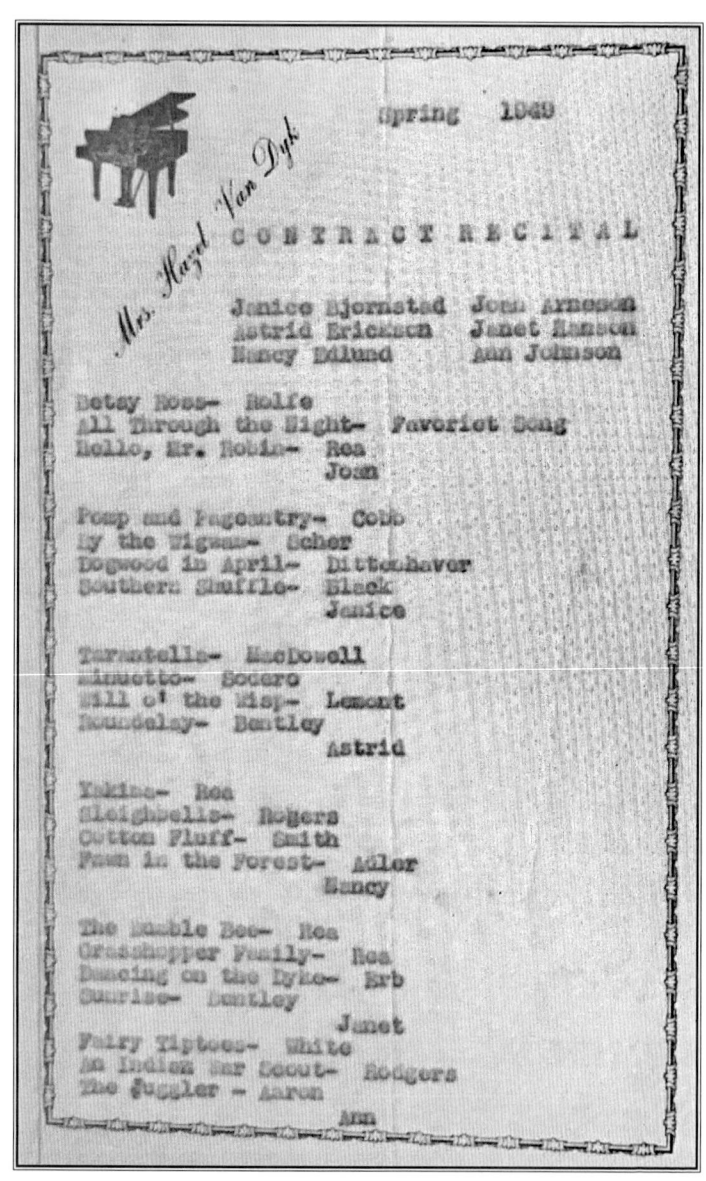

The Spring 1949 piano recital program at the home of Hazel Van Dyk. Piano student participants included Janice Bjornstad, Joan Arneson, Astrid Erickson, Janet Hanson, Nancy Edlund and Ann Johnson.

Chapter Eleven

McKinley School

DAVID FLEMING'S MEMORIES

"During first and second grade, I walked to McKinley School from my house at 1007 West Summit Avenue, a journey of about four blocks. I remember entering from the east side of the building," says David Fleming, FFHS Class of 1966.

David, classmate Tom Hintgen and some others from around town at other schools in addition to McKinley, transferred as third graders in the fall of 1956 to the new Our Lady of Victory Catholic School.

As for McKinley School, David Fleming vividly recalls a fairly steep hill running to the east where kids would slide in the winter months during recess. "That hill has been long removed," said David in January 2020.

He remembers that the playground had slides, monkey bars, swings and other play things made with pipe and steel.

"The ground was dirt and sand," he recalled, "and the result was more than one bump and bruise. But I remember the playground being great fun."

During the 1950s the front door at McKinley School was on the south side, on the 700 block of West Laurel Avenue. Kids also could enter on the east side of the building, and those doors were used during recess.

David says that kickball was very popular at McKinley School during the mid-1950s.

"As far as I remember, supervision or organization of play time by the school was almost non-existent. However, I think what we had for fun back then was more fun than what many kids have today in their structured and controlled play environment."

Fleming is like many people from that era who attended McKinley School who remember the gym as big during their youth, but small when adulthood arrived.

"Years later, when I had a job with Fergus Plumbing, I painted lots of pipe in the school, including the McKinley gymnasium. By then I realized this was a much smaller gym."

He remembers being a student at McKinley when the gym was a multi-purpose room, used for physical education, lunch and whatever.

"I distinctly remember getting my polio shot in the gym," Fleming recalls. "I can still see the line getting smaller and smaller as I was getting closer to the needle."

He also remembers, at the head of the room, the teachers and principal were at the table reserved for them for lunch time. "No private lounge for them."

His first-grade teacher was Miss Benson.

"I remember her as very kind," David said, "and I still have the class photo."

He recalls that for Valentine's Day, Miss Benson made a "mailbox" cardboard chest of drawers with each student's name. There was a big mail slot that read "Valentines."

Fleming and Hintgen still have photos of the cardboard post office with classmates also in the picture.

Mary Formick, referred to by most kids as "Miss Mary," was a popular second grade teacher at McKinley School.

"She was kind and we all liked her very much," Fleming recalled. "A few times she would take us out of class for a walk to a park."

David remembers his mother, Mae Fleming, during his second grade year making Christmas cookies to bring to Miss Mary for distribution to the students.

"Mom told me to be careful because they were sugar cookies and could be easily broken," he said. "During the walk to school, from West Summit Avenue, I dropped the cookies. I knew at that moment that I failed to bring them to Miss Mary intact. I felt guilty but could not tell my mother about the broken cookies."

McKinley School second grade class, 1955-56
Teacher Mary Formick, upper right

After his transfer as a third grader to Our Lady of Victory School, he remembers one year when Mary Formick, his former teacher, paid a visit to OLV. "She recognized me, and I felt good about that."

Fast forward to 2020. Fleming recalled the McKinley School days as a retiree wintering with his wife, Paulette, in Fountain Hills, Arizona, after a successful accounting career.

"I feel very fortunate to have grown up in Fergus Falls," he says.

Summers are spent in White Bear Lake near the Twin Cities and close to their daughter and family in Dellwood. David and Paulette spend lots of time with their two grandchildren.

They also spend time at a rustic cabin in Otter Tail County with family members.

MARLENE NELSON RUPP

In May 2021, while marking her 73rd birthday, Marlene Nelson Rupp became reflective while recounting her life's blessings.

The Twin Cities resident looked back on her growing up years in Fergus Falls, including her days at McKinley School.

"My parents built a home on Beech Avenue," she said. "They had five acres behind the house which bordered the State Hospital farmland."

The Nelson family had a little barn that housed one cow and some chickens. Later, the cow was switched out for two horses, which Marlene's sister and her friend enjoyed for several years.

"My parents had huge gardens, so I grew up learning to work first and then play," Marlene said.

She and her sister walked or biked everywhere.

"We lived a half mile from McKinley School and even walked home for lunch. The newspaper would list the weekly lunch menu. Getting to stay for hot lunch was a real treat. The turkey dinner and sloppy joes were favorites."

She fondly remembers recess, both during the school day and over the long lunch hour.

Marlene remembers each of her elementary teachers, but the memories of her second-grade teacher are particularly endearing. "Miss Mary (Formick) was an excellent teacher who had a kind, quiet, gentle manner and a warm smile."

Only one time was Marlene "called in" to see Miss Chelgren, the McKinley School principal.

"I went to the principal's office literally shaking with fear and trembling," she said, "not knowing what I had done wrong."

Several of the girls had chosen to do summersaults down the small hill on the northwest side of the school.

"An older neighbor lady observed through her window that when we did those summersaults, our panties showed. That was our crime."

Marlene recalls her elementary school years studying spelling words and doing math problems for homework. "I especially disliked long division," she said.

"Fights and discipline problems were never an issue. The teachers would even take short coffee breaks, and we dutifully did our classwork without any supervision."

She walked along the railroad tracks to get to Washington Junior High School just north of downtown Fergus Falls on Cavour Avenue. "I learned how to read the railroad lights so as not to be on the tracks when a train was approaching," Marlene recalled. "I had over a mile to walk to Roosevelt High School, too. I walked along the tracks for part of the walk. Then I took the north side of Lake Alice in the morning and walked home with friends on the south side of the lake after school."

She remembers having lots of homework every night for both her junior high and senior high years.

"Fergus had a great band program under Al Jacobs," Marlene said. "Marching band, concert band, and pep band were a huge part of my life."

Marlene, a 1966 FFHS grad, recalls that boys were involved in organized sports. They had not yet been established for girls during her high school years.

"Fifty-plus years ago, many of us were involved in our church youth groups. For me it was confirmation, Luther League, and summer Bible camps."

The Nelson house was one of the only homes that did not have a television.

"This was personally humiliating and embarrassing," she said, "but years later I would come to realize I learned to study and had more hours for practicing the piano and flute because I didn't have the distractions of watching TV."

Marlene says much has changed in our culture and society since growing up during the 1950s and 1960s.

"It's easy to reflect on an almost idyllic childhood, and in many ways, it was. I was so blessed."

1953 McKinley 5th grade intercity championship basketball team
Front, l-r: Paul Sigelman, Larry Dorn, Willie Thorddal; Back l-r:
Ron Dahl, Dick Peterson, Mike Loken, Ed Darby, Gene Shuck

Chapter Twelve

Stock Farm, Western Township

DAVE STOCK'S MEMORIES

David Stock, a member of the Fergus Falls High School class of 1966, grew up near the town of Western (later known as Western Township), located in the very southwest corner of Otter Tail County.

David Stock

"Our farm was 12 miles southwest of Fergus Falls and 12 miles northwest of Wendell," Dave said. "In Wendell, my father banked, sold cream, delivered grain, bought insurance and occasionally had farm repairs done at Aamot Implement, the International dealership. "

His parents were Henry T. and Marie Stock. Dave has four siblings.

As a youngster, Dave could purchase an ice cream cone at the Wendell pool hall and bought candy at Erickson's hardware store.

"But Wendell wasn't our town," he said. "We had an RFD #4, Fergus Falls address, and our sports loyalty was with the Fergus Falls Otters. A trip to Fergus Falls was an organized endeavor, and with three uncles who also lived and farmed in Western Township, these outings were often structured to meet the needs of many families."

The Stock families had several social outlets in Western, mainly the District #56 school that housed 1st through 8th grade.

"It was much like a home school today," Dave recalls. "When I was in 2nd grade, 8 of the 14 students were Stocks, and the teacher was my father's sister.

Kids enjoyed playtime outside at Western Township School District #56.
Photo courtesy of Otter Tail County Historical Society

"The other kids, the Ewerts and Jorgensons, have been life-long friends. The Munsons moved to California that year, and we never saw those kids again."

He says that the biggest school event was the annual Christmas program.

"The excitement of memorizing for the plays and your single recitation for the community event staged shortly before Christmas brought butterflies to your stomach," he said. "We also had a spring field day where we hosted two neighboring schools, #49 and #252. We knew some of the kids from these schools, but none very well unless they attended Western Presbyterian Church, a small community congregation."

A typical group of students at Western Township School District #56

Western Presbyterian didn't have the social network of District #56; mainly just church and Sunday School.

"We also had a Christmas program at the church, but nothing like the pageantry of the school program," Dave says. "The church was a place where you got to know some of the older folks from Western. We grouped them into two categories: Democrats or Republicans."

Dave's father was proud to be a Democrat and member of the Farmers Union. Members of the Farm Bureau were mostly Republicans.

"I was conflicted, because most of them (Republicans) seemed like nice people, with the exception of my great aunt (a Republican and Dave's Sunday School teacher), who made light of the fact that my father worked on Sundays."

There was also a German Lutheran church across the road where Dave's grandparents attended church.

To Dave, this church seemed cold and uninviting, and he doesn't recall ever going there.

In that same triangle was the Western Town Hall. He believes it thrived in an earlier time, when the Farm Bureau and Farmers Union both met there.

"The Farmers Union had a summer camp near Alexandria. We were picked up in Fergus by a Greyhound-type bus with 'Farmers Union' lettering on the side. At camp, we sang, 'I'm in the Union and I'm in to stay,' and returned believing the 'co-op way' was for all farmers."

He said the best social aspect of Western was the "Western Store" operated by Arnie Evenson, a single man divorced from his wife, Grace. He sold groceries, gas, beer and ice cream cones.

In later years, he offered a pool table, an evening attraction during Dave's early adolescence.

"Our greater family were teetotalers, so going to the store to drink beer wasn't in my uncles' constitution, and women never drank there," Dave said. "Some of the neighbors and even more men from outside the township would come down on a summer evening and tip back a few Hamm's®, Schmidt® or Grain Belt beers."

Dave's cousin, Mark, spent many summer evenings with Dave, shooting pool and drinking 10-cent Squirt® with 5-cent Planters® nuts mixed in. Pool games were 10 cents per cue.

"We figured out how to get value on slow evenings by having the owner, Arnie, join in our games," Dave said. "With four players, the high and low partnered after the red balls were gone."

It seemed like Mark would get Arnie as a partner often. Mark was a good actor and storyteller and would throw the game so he and Arnie would lose. Arnie was half the team.

"It cost the rest of us 10 cents collectively," Dave said. "I can still see the look on Arnie's face when Mark would blow a shot."

He said the store thrived during hunting season and when Abe Ewert organized a softball game in his pasture across the road.

"Unfortunately, Arnie's inventory of groceries was often stale and more expensive than 'George's' in Fergus, so by 1964 it closed permanently," Dave recalls. "Arnie was a good man (political persuasion unknown), who later remarried and ran a restaurant in Underwood."

Nowadays when a major storm is moving in, the weather bureau often refers to "Western" as a location in the path of the storm. Dave thinks back to those summer evenings and the fun he and others had at the Western Store.

Today the Stock farm headquarters remains at the same location where Dave grew up. While his mailing address is in Western, he and his wife, Debbie, reside at Otter Tail Lake. The town of Western, where his grandfather Herman was so proud to raise nine children, has no Stocks populating its six-square-mile area.

Chapter Thirteen

Lincoln School

BOB DRECHSEL'S MEMORIES

"We lived literally steps from Lincoln School. I could get to school in less than a minute if I wanted to," says Bob Drechsel, FFHS Class of 1967.

Bob lived at 423 North Union Avenue, just north of the railway overpass bridge, on the west side of the street. Lincoln School was a block away, to the north of the Drechsel home and also on the west side of the street, at 511 North Union.

The school was at the intersection of Union Avenue and Spruce, a street that headed westward from Union Avenue.

"I loved that school – the wood floors, the huge windows (one of which I once accidentally broke with an errant kickball), the cloak halls, the smell of polish and cleaning materials, and the overall warmth of the old building."

"I remember having good teachers in every grade, and there was remarkable stability in the teaching staff over the years." Bob's mother went to Lincoln School in the late 1920s and early 1930s. She and Bob had the same second grade teacher – Mildred Sparby.

Lincoln School on North Union Avenue was a landmark in Fergus Falls until the early 1980s. Photo [# 12054] from the collections of the Otter Tail County Historical Society.

"Miss Sparby was a great teacher," Drechsel said, "and she also always had a bird feeder outside of one of her classroom windows. I think that's one reason I love feeding birds to this day."

The music teacher, Bernice Roysland, would visit classrooms on a regular basis, and Fran Conito provided physical education.

"It was a warm and supportive environment, but you could count on being disciplined appropriately if you got out of line," Drechsel said.

"There was a huge asphalt playground surrounding the building on three sides – at least it seemed huge at the time. Playground equipment, probably all of which would be regarded as too dangerous today, took up about half of the grounds. There was room for kickball and other games on the rest of the grounds."

Each spring students enjoyed a Maypole dance on the playground, with an audience of parents and others.

"It was a sad day when the school was torn down. I still have a Lincoln School commemorative coffee mug, and use it to this very day," Drechsel said.

The annual Maypole dance at Lincoln School in 1959 was held at a corner of the old school. Photo courtesy of Bob Drechsel

"I see that Fergus Falls now has a new Lincoln School, but I don't think anything can replace the original."

The new Lincoln School is in the former Target building on the west side of town, to be used for early childhood education.

Drechsel, a University of Minnesota graduate, formerly wrote for the Daily Journal in Fergus Falls. He later taught in the journalism department at the University of Wisconsin. He and wife, Lynn, are retired and living in Madison, Wisconsin.

DANNY LOOMER'S MEMORIES

"I have an article from 5th grade basketball where we (Lincoln School players) won the intercity 5th grade basketball championship with a 12-0 record," said Danny Loomer, retired and living in southern California. "My teammates were Daryl Soliah, Tim Johnson, Paul Bang, Don Balfour, Roger Bjorklund, Jim Nash, Richard Lysne, John Severn and John Morstad."

Also, Lincoln won football and hockey championships that same year. Loomer's mother kept all the articles for Danny in a scrapbook.

Loomer, who later moved with his family to California where he graduated from high school, was also a member of the 1960 Fergus Falls VFW state championship baseball team coached by Oats LeGrand.

He later played minor league baseball as an infielder in the California Angels organization.

"Lincoln School was a wonderful place with terrific teachers, some of whom taught my father," says Severn.

A footnote: John Severn, a classmate of Loomer, lived right across the street from Lincoln School on North Union Avenue. Severn, in Chapter 14, talks about his grade school days and growing up years in Fergus Falls.

TREASURE HUNT ENDS AT LINCOLN SCHOOL

In the early 1960s, the Fergus Falls Chamber of Commerce sponsored a city-wide summer treasure hunt.

Clues appeared in the *Daily Journal*, and also were aired on the local radio station. There were about ten prizes of varying amounts from $10 to $25, and a grand prize of $50.

Medallions were hidden in public places, taped under park benches, at public buildings and other locations.

The final clue for the grand prize was, "between a president and a rocky shore."

That clue drew a person to Lincoln School on North Union Avenue. The searcher of the medallion surmised that "rocky shore" referred to the nearby west shore of Lake Alice.

Sure enough, that person found the medallion for the $50 grand prize underneath the outdoor entry mat to the east door of Lincoln School. He brought the medallion into the Chamber office and obtained the $50 grand prize.

LINCOLN SCHOOL HISTORY

The following information about Lincoln School, Fergus Falls, came from the Otter Tail County Historical Society. Included is an article printed in the April 6, 1905, issue of the *Fergus Falls Weekly Journal*. The headline read, "The best school building thus far erected here is formally opened."

Lincoln School was constructed at a cost of $83,373. The structure stood near North Union Avenue, north of the railway overpass bridge, until the early 1980s.

An open house was held on a Friday evening in the spring of 1905, with more than 1,000 people in attendance. Teachers welcomed guests to different rooms, the interior of the building exhibited several American flags and the school superintendent and school board members were the official hosts.

A framed picture of President Lincoln was prominently displayed. Light refreshments were served to visitors.

The new Lincoln School, a two-story structure in Fergus Falls, had 10 rooms and five stairways.

Those arriving to inspect the new school were impressed with the outside of the structure that included a stone foundation, mottled-pressed bricks, a broad green roof and impressive belfry.

The lower level had good lighting and afforded playrooms, storage rooms and a large area for the heating unit. Inside floors of Lincoln School were maple and window casings and general wood work was oak.

The heating and ventilation system was described by the head custodian:

"The school building is heated by steam and the ventilating system is one of the best obtainable. Fresh air comes in through large apertures, is heated to the desired temperature, and passes into the different rooms."

The total heating unit in 1905 cost $3,205 and plumbing costs amounted to $2,005.

Chapter Fourteen

John Severn Memories

JOHN SEVERN'S MEMORIES

During the days of sequestration related to COVID-19, John Severn says his mind often turned to his coming of age in Fergus Falls.

"This tendency was only reinforced by watching my grandchildren grow up in the 21st century," said Severn, a 1966 graduate of Fergus Falls High School.

John Severn

"I think I was three years old when we moved into the house at 612 North Union Avenue in Fergus Falls. My memories are tied to that house."

"The best thing about our house was that just behind it lived Jeanne Larson, my dear childhood playmate. The kitchen of the Larson house looked across to the kitchen of the Severn house. When each family sat down to dinner in the evening, we would wave to each other. Such a warm feeling."

"I remember in those early years the only rule was not to cross Union Avenue alone. Otherwise, we were relatively free to roam."

Jeanne and John confined their play time mostly to the back yards and their houses.

"When we began school a whole new world opened up," Severn said.

This brings John to the second best thing about his house.

"It was directly across the street from Lincoln School. There were, of course, patrol boys making the crossing of Union a safe proposition and we did not need adult accompaniment."

He says that Lincoln School was a wonderful place with terrific teachers, some of whom taught his father, Ken Severn, who later became a dentist. When the school was torn down in the early 1980s, Ken was given the old bell that at one time called students into class.

"I especially remember Miss Sparby, Mrs. Johnson and Miss Bratt," says John. "Such a secure place."

Recess was especially good, and John still has mental images of Danny Loomer driving the kickball over the back fence. "Danny was everyone's hero – incredibly athletic and a genuinely nice person and good friend. We were broken hearted when he moved to California."

Other good friends emerged in these years, including Roger Bjorklund, John Morstad, Nancy Van Dyken and Jane Hogen, to name a few. Bicycles were the main mode of transportation; there was no need for parents to drop kids off anywhere. "You were on your own," John emphasized.

In those days, there were no warnings about not talking to strangers. There were no strangers, other than the occasional patient from the state hospital walking by.

"My family moved out to Otter Tail Lake in the summertime, so I didn't take part in the summer activities of the city," John said. "Life at the lake was gloriously independent. We were free to roam all day if we wished, with only breaks for lunch and dinner."

His father commuted daily to his dental office in Fergus Falls. Severn family members at the lake had no car, no phone, no TV. That remained true until John left home for college.

"Junior high brought some changes. Washington Junior High School was three blocks south, just off Union, and I walked to it with my father every day as he made his way to work. Rain or snow."

He does not recall any occasion when he was driven to school. Severn adds that junior high marked a significant change in the routine of school, in that he and fellow classmates passed from room to room.

"My most prominent memory of Washington Junior High was the large study hall, always presided over by one dictatorial teacher or another always on the lookout for the

Washington School stood north of downtown Fergus Falls until 1967.

occasional whisper or the passing of notes," John said. "These were sins superseded only by the chewing of gum."

His next most prominent memory is that of gym class under the tutelage of Odis "Oats" Legrand. He ran a tight ship, and if one stepped out of line he got 'The Paddle.'

The routine was bend over, grab your ankles and smack. After this punishment, the student signed his name on the paddle. The other thing about gym was that students had to take showers afterwards.

His most memorable teacher was Len Rendz. Another thing about junior high, notes Severn, was that it served as a melting pot. Students from all over the city came under one roof from the various elementary schools: Lincoln, Cleveland, Jefferson, Madison, Adams, McKinley, Eisenhower and Our Lady of Victory.

"We were very patriotic in Fergus Falls," he said. "As a consequence one's circle of friends widened considerably. I became close friends with Tom Olson and Tom Johnson. And there were a lot of girls I had never seen before."

As for activities, there were organized sports, Boy Scouts, church groups, etc., but he remembers most the ice skating on Lake Alice in the winter months.

"I could put on my skates in the back hallway at our house and walk down to the lake, through the Larson's yard. The rink was lit, and there was the wonderful warming house presided over by an employee of the park department who kept the fire stoked and tightened your skates."

He also recalls the Lake Alice refreshment stand inside the warming house, run by the Townsends. There was music piped out to the rink. Kids gathered in small and sometimes large groups on Friday and Saturday nights, and boys and girls cautiously eyed one another.

"It was also in these years I began to ski – facilitated again by the park department, which ran Old Smokey on the south side of town. It was a good hill and you were transported to the top by two rope tows, a fast one and a slow one. At the bottom of the hill there was again a warming house."

It was at Old Smokey where Severn got his first lesson on racial tolerance.

"Often on Sundays, the Wahpeton Indian School brought a bus load of students over to ski. On this occasion, my brother Chuck was home from college and we were all out skiing. I worshiped my brother, who was nine years older than me."

John had skied down the hill and was waiting in line at the rope tow when one of the students from the Indian

School jumped the line. Severn yelled out, "Hey, Running Bear, you can't do that."

When he got to the top of the hill his brother Chuck was waiting.

"Chuck grabbed me by the collar, lifted me off the ground and said: 'Don't you ever let me hear you call someone a name like that again.' Lesson learned. I was shaken to the core."

John says that if this sounds idyllic, it was. It was just that he didn't know it at the time.

"Tenth grade brought real change – high school, in this case at Roosevelt Senior High School. For me, the walk to school lengthened appreciably, from three blocks to eight, though it shortened a bit in the winter when I could walk across Lake Alice."

He recalls that everything seemed bigger in senior high and a little more complicated. Academics became more challenging, relationships more stressful and athletics more consequential.

"Tenth grade marked the year you began driving, and that of course meant more freedom and more opportunity for trouble. In tenth grade I was still physically quite small, so the sports that suited me best were wrestling and tennis."

He participated in football, strongly encouraged by his parents.

There would also be new friendships that included Bobby Neumann and David Stigen along with the old ones.

"For the most part, I was an indifferent student but did well enough to avoid trouble at home."

Severn, in 11th and 12th grade, became socially more active but remained on the shy side.

"I hung out mostly with David Stigen and Tom Johnson, because the three of us did not have girlfriends. The teenage years were a bit more restrictive, because in Fergus Falls it seemed that everyone knew your business."

He remembers on one occasion driving the family car with friends, making the rounds from Dairyland to A&W root beer and passing by Skogmo's Café in downtown Fergus Falls.

"When I arrived home, I found my father standing at the top of the driveway waiting for me. He had received a phone call stating that I had been driving too fast down Vernon Avenue. That ended my evening."

"I had great parents, but they maintained strict curfew times that were earlier than any of my friends. That embarrassed me, and as a result I self-limited some of my social activities."

John said he never had a "birds and the bees" talk with his dad, but on one occasion his father took him aside and said: "Remember son, your mom and I have to live in this town." He got the drift.

"One of my fondest memories of these years was duck hunting with my father. During the season we would get up early and go out to Swan Lake where a group of men, including my father, had a hunting pass. We would shoot for 30 or 40 minutes, then hightail it back to town to get ready for school and work. Great fun."

Another lasting memory involved wrestling, which was a winter sport.

School didn't get out until 4 p.m., so wrestling practice started at 4:30. That meant that by the time Severn had showered and headed for home, it was nearly 7 p.m.

"The walk home was dreadful, and by the time I had trudged across Lake Alice and arrived home I was frozen to the bone and near starvation."

"My mother was a great cook and we ate like kings. There were dances at the armory, and David and I would spend the night walking the dance floor on the periphery trying to work up the nerve to ask a girl to dance."

High school teachers he remembers include Pearl Berge, Grace Halcrow, J. Arthur Johnson, Dale Ruehle, Earl Engan, Loren Woolson and Paul Anderson.

"But most importantly, I remember my wrestling coach, Dick Green. He was a truly fine man who cared so much for his athletes."

"I must confess, my high school years were not my finest moment, and that's not just my opinion."

"At my father's funeral 25 years ago, I saw Loren Woolson and Paul Anderson talking to one another, each smiling. So I went over and asked what was so amusing. They said they had just been talking and both concluded that I would have been the last of their former students that they would have picked out as going on to get a PhD."

Severn agreed with them. "But this is not to say that I didn't love growing up in Fergus Falls and on Union Avenue. I am who I am because of it."

He says Fergus Falls was like a warm blanket and it gave Severn the freedom to grow.

"Fergus Falls continues to occupy a prominent place in my heart. I return every summer to our cottage on Otter Tail Lake. Getting together with my lifelong best friend David Stigen is the highlight of my year."

Chapter Fifteen

State Hospital Farm

SUE WILKEN'S MEMORIES

For many years, the Fergus Falls State Hospital – later known as the Regional Treatment Center (RTC) on the north side of town – had its own farm.

"The complex had a complete farm with machinery, fields and livestock," said Sue Wilken, *Fergus Falls Daily Journal* columnist who worked at the Regional Treatment Center.

"My grandpa, Henry Hauptli, a former farmer, worked side by side with patients in the field," she said. "He believed that farm work was excellent therapy for them."

According to Wilken, many found a purpose in farm work and felt needed. "Grandpa believed that caring for the livestock helped many of the men battling depression."

The state hospital campus also boasted a large kitchen that was fully stocked.

"Much of the food was produced right on the campus," Wilken said. "Old timers raved about the homemade pickles that were offered on a regular basis."

The stock barn at the Fergus Falls State Hospital
Photo (# 34041) from the collections of the
Otter Tail County Historical Society

In the early days, everything was made from scratch.

"The state hospital smelled wonderful when bread was baking," Wilken said. "In 1976, the food was excellent. There was still a baker who took great pride in his pies."

In the cafeteria, called the 'congregate dining room', employees and patients shared tasty meals.

"There also was a beauty shop, barbershop, canteen, gymnasium and woodworking shop for vocational training," Wilken recalls.

In the early days, the people at the state hospital were called patients because it was, in fact, a hospital.

"During my days as an employee, people were called residents because it was their home," she said.

"I will always recall the laughter and tears as we at the state hospital cared for and loved people who struggled with their disabilities. Those were the days."

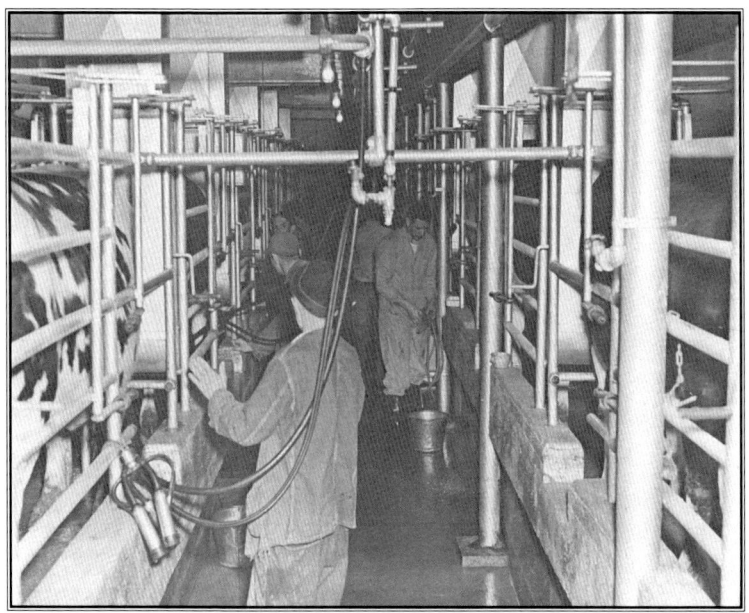

Dairying at the Fergus Falls State Hospital. The man with his back to the camera is Gilbert Opsahl. Photo (# 34042) from collections of the Otter Tail County Historical Society.

STATE HOSPITAL WAS ONCE HOME TO COMMUNITY COLLEGE

Fergus Falls Junior College, later known as the community college, was located in the east wing of the state hospital in 1967-68 and moved to the new campus on the northwest side of Fergus Falls in the fall of 1968.

The move to the state hospital came about after the Washington School fire in late May 1967.

During the following school year, in 1967-68, the college wing at the high school was needed when split shifts accommodated junior and senior high school students.

The old fairgrounds became the site for construction of a new junior high to replace the destroyed Washington School. Darlene Rian, who in 2020 lived in the Twin Cities as a retired accountant, recalled Lee Krogh as the English and drama instructor at the junior college (state hospital east wing) in 1967-68.

Darlene, Rachel Hexum and Jean Ackerman were in one of Krogh's plays.

"It was so much fun and Lee was so creative in both writing us into the play and creating the theatre up in the rafters of the state hospital for the college year of 1967-68," Darlene said. "I totally enjoyed college at this other 'state institution' in Fergus. It was a real learning experience in many ways."

After the move to the new campus, some junior college students stayed at the state hospital while receiving board and room in exchange for work at the state hospital.

Chapter Sixteen

Linwood Court

DAN LARSON'S MEMORIES

"In 1958, my dad, Clarence (Butch) Larson, announced we would be moving to Fergus Falls from Richfield, Minnesota. He had been an Air Force recruiter in the metro area and would be doing the same in Fergus."

Clarence (Butch) and Irene Larson with their children, oldest to youngest: Dan, Nancy, Tim and Becky, circa 1963

"When you're 10, you don't argue, you just go where the folks say to go. So with the car loaded, we headed northwest to a new home."

But as Dan remembers, there was no new home as yet.

The Miller Brothers were building their new house in Linwood Court. It was a one-story, one garage unit overlooking cornfields in the back yard at that time.

The cul-de-sac was situated off Fir Avenue, a couple of blocks east of Union Avenue.

"One way in and one way out," Dan recalls. "You drove to the end where our house would be, drove around a circle of grass and concrete curbing, and street lights and back toward Fir Avenue."

"'The circle,' as we called it, was the preferred snow piling area for the city of Fergus Falls. We had to keep the fire hydrant clear."

While the Larson house was being built, the family had to spend at least a month at a small resort on West Battle Lake.

"We had swimming, fishing, and loved every minute of it," Dan recalls. "What a summer."

The family moved to their new home just before school started. Dan had time to meet kids from the neighborhood, such as Bob Kucera and Steve Larson.

The neighborhood had a variety of people in different lines of duty. There was a taxidermist four houses down from the Larsons, the Otter Tail Power fleet superintendent, a locally-famous music instructor, an elementary principal, a banker, a game warden, an insurance investigator and more.

"Ours was a great, close-knit neighborhood, especially with the annual Christmas light battle royale between the

The Christmas lights attracted many people to Linwood Court in the years following World War II.

neighbors. I sometimes wonder how many lights were actually lit annually by the Linwood Court faithful," Dan said.

He is pretty sure that Otter Tail Power, where his father later worked, loved the annual light display.

"It was like running a gauntlet of holiday lights, and it was impressive. Many wire reindeer, Santas, elves and stars were propped up in the snow."

One year his dad and mom, Irene, decided to collect money and canned goods for good causes and dressed like the Clauses for many nights. Below zero evenings were not uncommon, so it wasn't all fun. "The number of cars, bumper to bumper, easily numbered in the hundreds for a couple of hours each night during the Christmas season," Dan said.

"One year it was cold enough to prop up in the front yard an actual, once-living (before the annual deer season) whitetail deer dad had harvested some weeks before and kept frozen for a month. The line of cars viewing lights and donating the food and money were slowed considerably by the sight of a once-live deer, now bathed in a spotlight and with a red nose."

All the neighbors at the end of the court took turns taking care of the circle, keeping it mowed all summer long. Many summers, large plant containers would be sitting in the circle, full of annual flowers just to dress the place up a little, with half a dozen neighbors pitching in.

In the winter, the circle would be piled very high with lots of snow pushed up by the plows. High enough some years for Dan and his siblings, Nancy, Tim and Becky, to slide down on.

One year, one of the neighbors checked into purchasing flowering crab trees for the sidewalk areas that ran on both sides of the street.

"I'm pretty sure Butch Larson had something to do with this project," said Dan, "and getting the cost quotes for the trees. These trees are mostly still there and as far as I know, flower in the spring with those fantastic pink blossoms."

He remembers when a few of the neighbors balked at the price or didn't quite see the value of such a beautification project.

"Somehow they were convinced it was good for the neighborhood and good for their homes as well. All eventually participated. Christmas tree lights adorned them all in the light's heydays."

"The Larsons, Aunes, Germundsons, O'Briens, Metcalfs, Beckens, Eschweillers, Kuceras, Gails, Rendzs, Amdals and Mannings had a special neighborhood to raise families, enjoy many golden years and provide platinum memories for those descendants of a Linwood Court neighborhood."

LASTING FRIENDSHIPS

"I was the new kid on the block back in 1958. Linwood Court was being developed and we were lucky enough to be able to build a new house," recalls Dan Larson.

"I was a 6th grader that year at Cleveland School, and shortly after school started Fran Conito announced the 6th grade tackle football schedule, with all games to be played at the Athletic Park. That's where my first good friends were made, on that football team."

Larson said his team won each game because they had teammate Al Svare.

"Nobody could catch Al," Larson said. "He was the Crazy Legs Hirsch of the 1958 6th grade football league. Steve Larson and Bob Kucera lived about a block away from me, so we connected that summer."

Next was 6th grade basketball on the schedule.

"This was when I was introduced to the good basketball players around town and to guys who would remain good friends right to the present time," says Larson.

Len Rendz was the coach. Larson, Bob Warn, Curt Thompson, Charlie Christopherson, Dave Olson, Duane Jenson, Pete Ellingson and Bruce Josephs were just some of players the athletics brought together.

"We still get together whenever we can and talk about the good old days. These are valuable friendships forever."

MORE ABOUT THE LINWOOD COURT NEIGHBORS

Butch Larson (wife Irene) – Butch worked for Otter Tail Power Company (power production). Butch survived the Bataan Death March that began on April 9, 1942, during World War II in the South Pacific. He also survived the relocation of prisoners on ships, which he said were worse than the actual march. Butch survived 3½ years of captivity in brutal conditions.

John Aune (wife Bev) – John had a transport business.

Duane Larson (wife Mary) – Duane worked at Fergus Falls National Bank. Duane said he always remembered when his kids, Kathleen and James, opened the door and were greeted by Butch Larson dressed up as Santa during the holiday season.

Warren O'Brien (wife Phyllis) – Warren was a game warden.

Jim Metcalf (wife Dorothy) – Jim worked at Minnesota Motor Company.

Russ Becken (wife Marjorie) – Russ worked for Otter Tail Power (electric transmission).

Geneva Eschweiller – Geneva was an instructor and director of choral activities at Fergus Falls Community College.

Omer Germundson (wife Mary Ann) – Omer worked for Otter Tail Power (fleet service for company-owned cars and trucks).

Glen Kucera (wife Kathryn) – Glen worked for Otter Tail Power Company (power production).

Len Rendz (wife Marlys) – Len worked for Fergus Falls Public Schools.

Eugene Manning (wife Helen) – Eugene was a grade school principal.

Jim Amdal (wife Gladys) – Jim did law office investigative work. As part of Jim Amdal's obituary: "The Linwood Court neighborhood became very special. Neighbors quickly became lifelong friends, extra hands with home projects, coffee, dinner and camping companions, and co-Christmas lights displayers."

Duane Baglien, Fergus Falls Otter boys basketball coach, later sold his house at Linwood Court to John and Bev Aune before moving to Edina in 1957.

DUANE LARSON, 2019 HALL OF FAME INDUCTEE

In 2019 Linwood Court resident Duane Larson was inducted into the Fergus Falls High School Hall of Fame. Following is information from the induction program:

> **Duane Larson** *is a native of Fergus Falls, having graduated from Fergus Falls High School in 1945. Larson entered the music program in September 1937 at the age of 10 with Luther Onerheim as his first music and band instructor.*
>
> *During his school years, he was a member of the Junior and Senior High School bands. Larson also played in the Junior and Senior High School orchestras, pep band, marching band and the Dinner Ensemble, a small chamber group of students who played for various civic functions.*
>
> *From 1938 to 1940, Larson participated in the summer band camp at Fair Hills Resort. He was first chair flute for the combined bands when the camp closed in 1940 due to the start of World War II.*
>
> *During his high school years, Larson was fortunate to take lessons from Donald Berglund, later director of the St. Olaf Orchestra, William Pfeiffer, from the Cincinnati Conservatory, and Al Hapke, a retired musician from Chicago*

who would occasionally play with the Chicago Symphony.

After graduation, Larson enlisted in the Army Air Force and spent two years in military service.

He returned to Fergus Falls in 1947 and accepted a job at Fergus Falls National Bank, which he expected to be temporary employment. Forty-five years later, he retired from the bank and two years later he found part-time employment with West Central Initiative, where he has been for almost 25 years.

Upon returning to Fergus Falls in 1947, Frank Hedlund called to inform him he was forming the Fergus Falls Civic Orchestra and asked if Larson would be interested in playing in the group. He became a charter member of the orchestra and played for more than 50 seasons. Larson presently plays with the Heart of the Lakes Community Band, the M-State College and Community Band and the Fergus Falls Civic Orchestra. He has also appeared as a guest soloist with the Silver Winds Flute Choir of Hopkins.

Duane was a member of the National Flute Association and the Upper Midwest Flute Association. He died September 19, 2021.

Chapter Seventeen

Tomhave Farm

RICHARD TOMHAVE'S MEMORIES

Richard Tomhave, FFHS Class of 1965, was raised on a family farm just northwest of Fergus Falls. The exact location was north of Weyrens Road and a short distance from what today is Fleet Farm.

His parents were Roland and Louise Tomhave.

Roland was born June 22, 1912, the son of Albert and Myrtle Tomhave. They built a farm home the same year Roland was born. Roland attended country school through the eighth grade at the District 96 school, where the Fergus Falls ethanol plant is now located.

Originally, the farm included 120 acres. In addition to the house was a barn, hog house, chicken coop and machine shed.

Seven years after Roland's birth, on June 22, 1919, his parents and sisters Naomi, Elida and Erma were celebrating Roland's birthday. The celebration was quelled when they heard the news of the cyclone striking Fergus Falls, resulting in loss of life and destruction of property.

The barn and hog house at the Tomhave farm

Albert, in addition to operating the Tomhave farm, also operated a feedmill right on the farm. His specialty was grinding feed for area farmers. Included were corn and wheat.

"My father Roland, after taking over the farming operations, farmed with horses for many years," Richard said.

Roland's first tractor was a John Deere, purchased during the war years of the 1940s. He owned a threshing machine and used that for harvesting.

"Help was hard to come by during World War II, with many men fighting overseas," Richard said. "Local businessmen would come out to farms and help my father and other farmers shock grain."

One year, during the fall harvest, Roland was at a local filling (gas) station. He ran across four men who he later learned were wanted by law enforcement in Chicago.

Many years later Roland told Richard that the ring leader claimed to know all about horses. Roland hired the four men for some short-term work.

"One morning my father found the ring leader down at the barn harnessing a team of horses inside the barn," Richard said. "But there was only a single barn door, which the team of horses could not get through."

In 1958 the Tomhave crop was lost to a hailstorm.

"That's when my dad, in addition to farming, began many years working on construction," Richard said. "He farmed until the early 1970s and then rented the land."

Richard and his sister Mary, FFHS Class of 1962, were raised on the farm. Like their father, they attended the District 96 school.

Their mother, Louise (Piekarski), who married Roland on October 15, 1942, was great at making homemade beet pickles and sugared raised donuts. She helped manage the farm, and later on worked at a nursing home in Fergus Falls as an aide.

Canning time for Louise involved processing the garden produce, butchering chickens and picking eggs.

Richard and Mary recall many gatherings with aunts and uncles and their families. Amazingly, Roland and Mary each won cars – Roland at the county fair in 1940, and Mary at the Our Lady of Victory Church (OLV) fall festival in 1961.

In 1940, county fair tickets for car drawings were given out by merchants after people purchased goods at downtown business establishments. A certain number of tickets were given out for each dollar spent at the businesses.

Raffle tickets were sold in advance of the drawing for the car at OLV Church.

"Back then farm neighbors helped each other," Richard said. "When needs arose they were there for one another for haying, harvesting and you name it."

There were farm lunches made by Louise for hardy crews at threshing time.

He said that farm families "just getting together" had its special rewards. "I miss those good times when neighbors really knew neighbors."

MORE ABOUT TOMHAVE FARM ACTIVITIES

Roland Tomhave used dynamite to clear rocks and stumps from the land, said Richard.

One day his father-in-law, Frank Piekarski, who lived next door, told Roland, "You have to stop all the blasting because my chickens have stopped laying eggs."

Those were the days of not only grain farming but also diversified farming with cattle, hogs and chickens.

In the early years, the hay was put up loose by means of a hay loader. Years later, the neighbors helped bale the hay. Roland never owned a hay baler.

The Great Northern railroad tracks went through the Tomhave farm northwest of Fergus Falls. Residents of the State Hospital, later known as the Regional Treatment Center, would walk along the tracks.

One time there was a rainstorm and Roland got caught in the elements when he was plowing a field near the railway tracks. He had to unhook the plow and make a dash for home.

It took several days for the weather to change.

"Dad was wondering how rusty the plow would be," Richard said. "When he returned to the field, to his surprise, the plow was all greased and in great condition. It turns out that a state hospital patient had taken care of the plow for my dad."

Another neighbor had his plow left in the field, also. But the patient liked John Deere green and the neighbor's plow color was red. The red color was not much to the liking of the state hospital patient.

In his later years, after retiring from farming, Roland sold the farm machinery and started working at two rest areas along I-94.

More Farm Memories from Richard Tomhave

"While growing up on the farm, I remember the times the cousins and families would come for family gatherings," Richard said.

Roland told about the time when he was a child and climbed up onto the platform of the windmill on the farm to hide from his parents. It was Roland who first introduced Richard to cisterns, a below-ground cement structure for holding soft water for household use.

Pheasants on the farm: Richard remembers a local school principal and judge coming to the Tomhave farm. The judge flushed out several pheasant roosters. He was so excited that he forgot to pull the trigger, instead ejecting all of his shells without firing a shot.

He has many memories of fence lines, butchering cattle, straw piles from threshing, the short ride to town on the school bus, using a big drive-in barn, snow-plugged roads during the winter months, and a big garden for produce.

There was a large-sized slough on the farm. Duck hunting and goose hunting were great for many years.

"One time, Dad, me and a good friend of mine were goose hunting," Richard said. "We were taking a break when two geese came in flying low across the slough. Dad had a double-barrel shotgun, but it was empty."

"He promptly reached into his pocket for shells, pulled out what he thought were shells but then tried to load a roll of lifesavers into the gun. The geese flew right over us untouched."

Richard and Theresa Tomhave were married in 1977. That year they purchased the homestead and 14 acres. Roland and Louise moved into a new house built up the road but still near the farmstead.

Roland died in 2005 and Louise died in 2013.

Richard Tomhave in front of the Tomhave farmhouse which was built in 1912. The house, remodeled, is located northwest of Fleet Farm.

In 1990, the farmstead with buildings was sold and a new owner took over the farmsite. Richard and Theresa also built a new home up the road, but still close to the farm. They have two daughters, Stephanie and Amy, and six grandchildren.

Richard and Theresa later moved to the northeast section of Fergus Falls. Richard and his friends continued to hunt ducks and geese at the slough near the former Tomhave farmstead. As of 2021 the Tomhave farmland was still being rented out.

In closing, Richard points to a phrase from the Pioneer Heritage Conservation Trust: "The land goes on forever, leaving on it the marks of each existing landowner."

Chapter Eighteen

South Court, West Vasa

NEIGHBORHOOD MEMORIES

A prominent house at 620 South Court Street, on the northwest corner of Court and Vasa, was built in 1907 by Fred G. Barrows, who helped establish Otter Tail Power Company in 1909.

Many families have lived at the home built in 1907 by Fred G. Barrows.

Over the years, starting in the 1950s, some owners of this elegant home included Thomas and Dorothy Cashman, Tom and Barb Donoho, Wayne and Gloria Ronning, Don and Maryjane Westra, Don and Wanda Hogue and Jeremy and Sarah Brunn.

I remember attending a birthday party for Jerry Cashman at the house in 1957, when he and I were 3rd graders at Our lady of Victory School in Fergus Falls.

Thomas Cashman had a stock market home ticker tape machine in his house on South Court Street. That machine was the ancestor to the modern computer printer, transmitting text over a wire to a printing device.

Cashman sons, Tim and Dan, went into the tree business in western North Dakota – Tim in Minot and Dan in Bismarck. In college, Tim was a backup running back at the

Tim Cashman, a star Fergus Falls High School football running back who played with the winning Minnesota Gophers in the 1962 Rose Bowl, grew up at the house built by Fred Barrows during the 1950s.

University of Minnesota. He played in the 1962 Rose Bowl game in Pasadena, California, when the Gophers defeated UCLA 21-3.

In later years, Tim hosted hunting outings for his high school buddies Roger Sinner, John Soby, Andy Anderson, Tom Greenagel, Roger Hesby and others.

In 1960, I attended a Boy Scout patrol leader meeting at the Barrows house when it was occupied by Tom Donoho. He was scoutmaster for Troop 312, sponsored by the Knights of Columbus. Tom finished the meeting before the start of the first Nixon-Kennedy TV debate.

A block to the north, on the northwest corner of Court Street and Vernon Avenue, was the home of Dr. David Sanderson, Sr., and his wife, Margaret. Their eight children were David, Jr., Jane, Steve, Paul, Julie, Nancy, Robert and Sara.

All of the Sanderson kids were active in school activities. The parents enjoyed golf and other activities. Dr. Sanderson was an avid Minnesota Twins fan. Sadly, son Robert died in 1964 after a lengthy illness.

David Sanderson, Jr., and his close friend, Greg Peterson, were avid duck hunters.

Ralph and Gert Sinner and their sons, Gregg and Roger, lived on South Court Street where the boys grew up in the 1950s. Ralph was a pharmacist, who operated Johnson Drug in downtown Fergus Falls.

Gert Sinner and my mother, Claire, were first cousins. Roy and Claire Hintgen, Ralph and Gert Sinner, and Bob and Mae Fleming would often enjoy dining together at the Elks Club in downtown Fergus Falls on Saturday evenings in the 1950s and 1960s.

Son Roger Sinner was a star Otter all-around athlete, who later pitched in the San Francisco Giants minor league organization.

Roger Sinner grew up during the 1950s on South Court Street, here shown in uniform when he pitched in 1963 and 1964 for Tacoma as part of the San Francisco Giants organization.

Dayton and John Soby were in the neighborhood also, living at the northwest corner of South Mill Street and West Vasa Avenue. Their parents were B.K. Soby, a construction company owner, and his wife Lucile.

The basketball hoop and spacious driveway at the Soby home attracted lots of kids, including Roger Sinner, who joined the Soby kids and others for many hours of practice. This hard work paid off, with the Fergus Otters finishing 27-1 and taking third place at the state boys basketball tournament in 1957.

Today, Larry and Jeannette Dorn live across the street from the Barrows house on the southwest side of the intersection. In 1968, Larry became the owner of Dorn & Company, financial advisors.

Another house across from the Barrows house, at the northeast corner of Court and Vasa, was occupied by Judge Harlan Nelson and his wife, Inga, and later on by Erik and Lisa Ahlgren.

Inga Nelson was active as a swim coach.

Erik Ahlgren, an attorney, for several years operated Shoremaster, which was started by his late father-in-law, Dennis Tuel.

In later years, Wayne Horgen, his wife Marilyn and their four sons lived at the southeast corner of the intersection of South Mill and West Vasa. Wayne was the Otter boys and girls hockey coach and their sons played Otter hockey.

The former Soby home was later moved to the east side of town. This was necessary due to the construction of the new Lake Region HealthCare building.

LANCE JOHNSON MEMORIES

Lance Johnson, a 1956 graduate of Fergus Falls High School, first lived in a two-bedroom bungalow at 710 South Court Street, built in 1933 by the J.P. Construction Company, which was owned by his father's uncle.

Johnson's memories are included in his 2005 book, *Fergus Falls and the Fabulous Fifties.*

Later, the Johnson family moved to a home on the northeast corner of the intersection of South Court Street and West Vasa Avenue.

Lance's father, Leonard G. Johnson, became a partner with Reuben Peterson and Cliff Vigen in the Fergus Jobbing Company in 1930. They were a wholesaler of candy and tobacco products.

Leonard Johnson had a small woodshop in the basement of his house where he built toy cars out of wood.

The H.E. Swenson house was near the Leonard Johnson house. H.E. was a bank president and considered a pillar in the community of Fergus Falls. He and his wife had four children: Helmer, Jr., Mary, Fred and Bill.

Lance remembered H.E. inviting neighbor kids over to watch 8-mm movies.

He also remembers, as a kid, building pushmobiles, which were similar to soapbox racers.

"We would coast down Vasa Avenue, westward toward Union Avenue," noted Lance, "steering with either our feet or a crude steering wheel. We did our best to avoid cars, but it was a miracle that someone didn't get struck by a vehicle."

Johnson says that all the kids in the neighborhood appreciated having nice playmates.

For Christmas 1952, his parents gave Lance an antique reed organ. At the public library he found a March 1950 *Popular Mechanics* magazine, which told him how to motorize the old reed organ.

"I found myself repairing reed organs for others," he said, "and thus was born Johnson Organ Company."

He moved his business to Moorhead in 1967, and then to Fargo in 1971. Over the years, he has been widely known for playing the Mighty Wurlitzer at the Fargo Theater and also the Mighty Wurlitzer at A Center for the Arts in Fergus Falls.

DAYTON SOBY MEMORIES

During the 1940s and 1950s, there were dozens of young people who lived within the four square blocks which touched the intersection of South Court Street and West Vasa Avenue.

"That area became a center of activity," said Dayton Soby, a 1957 graduate of Fergus Falls High School.

Soby's father was B. K. Soby, who was a partner in the highway construction business known as the John Dieseth Company. He later started the Soby Construction Company.

B. K. was also a co-founder of Security State Bank and the M-R Sign Company. He and his wife, Lucile, were active in the community of Fergus Falls. B.K. was a leader of many community development projects and organizations.

Soby was among those who started the Fergus Area College Foundation in the early 1960s, which raised money for students attending the new junior college, today part of M State.

Young Lance Johnson lived at the northeast corner of the intersection of Court and Vasa. The back yard of the Johnson home was a fairly long hill, which extended down into the back yard of young Dayton Soby and his younger brother, John.

"In the winter, that hill became the center of activity," Dayton said. "Neighborhood kids came over with their sleds, their skis, and an occasional toboggan, to slide down the hill from the Johnson house to the Soby house."

Several kids would head down on a toboggan with others chasing to catch them with sleds, while all were trying to avoid crashing into several big trees on either side of the alley dividing the two lots. Injuries were minor.

Lance built a small scaffold at the top of the hill for skiers to get a faster start. He also built a big snow-ice bump, which was called a "ski jump," halfway down the hill. That's where skiers jumped for several feet on their way down. He also put up lights to enable this activity after dark.

Lance Johnson's father, Leonard Johnson, had a woodshop in his basement, and Lance became a skilled builder of many things.

"He started his eventual organ-building business, known as Johnson Organ Company, while in high school. Lance sold his first organ, a refurbished small pump organ with wood paneling, to our family," said Dayton Soby.

Another center of activity was "Soby's Court," a basketball court consisting of an enlarged driveway with a backboard and basket mounted on the garage, constructed by B. K. Soby for his sons Dayton and John.

"This was big enough for 3-on-3 ball," Dayton said. "Many dozens of players had fun playing basketball there for many years. In the winter we would shovel off the court and play basketball, sometimes with boots and mittens on. We had a light bulb hanging over the court, even playing after dark."

The core of the 1957-58 Otter basketball team, which almost made it to the state tournament, grew up on Soby's Court. Players included Roger Sinner, John Soby, Tom Greenagel and Peter Hoff. After their high school graduation, 1957 Otters all-state-tournament player Curt Reinan, along with classmates Dayton Soby, Gordy Jenson and Jonathan Preus, played countless 2-on-2 games.

All the kids around Court and Vasa went to Adams Grade School. Soby recalls that when he and his friends were young, the area east of Mill Street, across the street from his house, seemed like it was a foreign country since the kids on that side went to Madison Grade School.

By high school, Madison athletes such as Tom Glorvigen, Wally Swanson, Ed Darby, Gordy Jenson and Roger Hesby had crossed that line to Soby's Court and joined the Vasa/Court neighborhood.

MORE ABOUT THE BARROWS HOUSE

The house that Fred Barrows built in 1907 at 620 South Court Street represented a lifestyle that was the envy of many Fergus Falls residents.

There are three fireplaces of imported tile and one of brick. The dining room in the English Cottage-style house is paneled in oak, with leaded glass in the windows and a built-in china cupboard.

On the third floor, wrote Jim Gray in his book, *Building from the Past*, with co-author Marjorie Barton, is the former maid's room and bath.

This was and still is a large house, as witnessed by two bathrooms on the second floor. There was and is plenty of room to roam for children of the home owners and their friends.

An older, four-stall garage on the north side of the house was replaced with a more modern garage. The back porch has also been remodeled.

MORE ABOUT DON AND MARYJANE WESTRA

Many times, it is mentioned that a Fergus Falls resident who has passed away leaves a legacy that will live on in Fergus Falls. In the case of Don Westra, who died at the age of 69 on December 21, 2019, his legacy will live on – not only locally, but also where he did good work in the countries of Zimbabwe and Honduras.

Locally, Westra, who lived in the Fred Barrows house, will best be remembered as the founder of West Tool & Design, still managed by his son, Evan, on the northwest side of Fergus Falls.

Don and his wife, Maryjane, and their children enjoyed living at the Barrows' house. Don was a charter member and past president of the Tri-State Manufacturers Association, and past president of the Fergus Falls Economic Improvement Commission.

He lived a dream, alongside his wife Maryjane, by volunteering through Global Ministries after retirement.

Don helped people build a better life through farming and well drilling in Zimbabwe, a country in South Africa. It was there where, as a Fergus Falls Rotarian, he helped establish Zimbabwe's Chipinge Rotary Club.

Don also shared his knowledge and expertise with vocational education in Honduras, a country in Central America, in the community of Yoro.

"He left things better than he found them," said the Rev. Douglas Dent during Don's funeral at Federated Church, Fergus Falls. "One example is how Don worked in providing clean water for people in Zimbabwe."

Reflecting on Don as a warm and compassionate person, while providing personal insights into his many good works, were Dean Eggermont and Rud Wasson.

"It took courage and determination from both Don and Maryjane to work in conditions of poverty, corruption and inefficiencies," Wasson said.

Chapter Nineteen

Pederson Farms

PEDERSON MEMORIES

Curt Pederson, a member of the Fergus Falls High School Class of 1965, and his brother Les, a member of the FFHS Class of 1966, have good memories of growing up on two farms in Buse Township, south of Fergus Falls.

Their parents were LeRoy and Corinne (Vore). There were six children: Larry, Carol, Curt, Les, Linda and Cay.

LeRoy, Corinne and their children enjoyed living on the two family farmsteads in Buse Township. LeRoy farmed until 1965, when he went to work for the Fergus Bus Company. He was 79 when he died in 2004.

Today Don Pederson, uncle of Curt and Les Pederson, lives on the first Pederson farmstead in Buse Township. This site was the first homestead for Curt and Les Pederson before moving to the second farmstead two miles from Dayton Hollow School.

Horses were used on the Pederson farms in Buse and Tordenskjold townships.   Photo courtesy of Curt Pederson

Curt and Les' grandparents were Henry and Nettie (Forde) Pederson. Henry was born in 1894 in Buse Township, the son of Hans and Mary (Anderson) Pederson.

Henry lived and farmed there his entire life. He died at the age of 85 in 1979. He served on the Agricultural Stabilization and Conservation Service (ASCS) and the Otter Tail Co-op Oil board for several years,

Curt Pederson's family ties include not only the Pederson family, but also the Forde-Botts families. The families have ties to Norway and Sweden from the old country.

Another family farm was located in Tordenskjold Township (Underwood), where Hans and Mary Pederson are buried.

above: Curt Pederson in front of the barn in 2021 at the second family farmsite where he was raised in Buse Township, two miles from the Dayton Hollow country school.

right: Les Pederson in 2021, with grandsons Clayton, left, and Eli, at the farmsite of his grandparents, Henry and Nettie (Forde) Pederson, where Les now resides.

DAYTON HOLLOW SCHOOL, WESTERN STORE REMEMBERED

As they approached their 55th class reunion in 2021, some members of the Fergus Falls High School Class of 1966 recalled their attendance at the Dayton Hollow School south of Fergus Falls.

"Sharyl Auseth, Les Pederson and I came to 9th grade at the old junior high (Washington School) after attending Dayton Hollow School from grades one through eight," said Jim Rasmusson, FFHS Class of 1966.

"In the late 1950s and early 1960s, the enrollment at Dayton Hollow School ranged from 16 to 24 students," Rasmusson said.

The Dayton Hollow School was among the classic country schools in Otter Tail County.
Photo courtesy of Donna Ohe

Curt Pederson, FFHS Class of 1965 and the older brother of Les Pederson, also attended Dayton Hollow School. He also remembers the historic Western Store, south of Dayton Hollow in southwestern Otter Tail County.

The store, which operated two miles south of Orwell Dam, was built in 1897 and operated until 1964.

It was a place to not only purchase items such as a spool of thread, a bar of soap and kerosene, but also a place to visit with friends, especially on summer evenings.

"Farm families in Western Township could run in and stop at the Western Store for anything from soup to nuts," said Pederson.

Shortly before the store closed, a staff writer for the *Fergus Falls Daily Journal* reported that "little changed through the years, although of late the old cracker barrel disappeared, a new gas pump was installed and coolers were added for cold meats and milk."

A 1930's-vintage beer sign stood until the closing of the store.

Owners during the 65 years of the Western Store included the Kritzers, Packards, Meyers and Loomers. Renters included the Hubbards, Holts and Petersons. Arnold Evenson took over in 1948 and ran the store until 1962.

Chapter Twenty

West End Grocery

JIM GERHARDSON'S MEMORIES

Otto Gerhardson was the grandfather of 1957 Fergus Falls High School graduate Jim Gerhardson. It was Otto who built and operated the West End Grocery at the southeast corner of West Cavour Avenue and Buse Street in Fergus Falls. Running the grocery store with Otto was his wife, Hilma.

"There was a gas pump in front of the store," said Jim, now a resident of the Twin Cities. "My parents, Helmer and Ruth Gerhardson, took over ownership late in 1949. I worked at the store for nine years, starting at age nine until I enlisted in the Army."

West End Grocery offered kerosene, which the Gerhardsons hand-pumped in the office part of the store, until people stopped buying it. More and more people started purchasing electric kitchen stoves.

"That was a time when people were converting to electric stoves and they could afford the conversion," he said. "How my mother cooked for our family on a two-burner kerosene stove still amazes me."

*West End Grocery was also known as Gerhardson's Grocery
on West Cavour Avenue, a block west of Broadway.*

West End Grocery also provided free home delivery and was open seven days a week.

"I remember being interrupted during many Sunday dinners to sell something that our customers had forgotten to buy during the week," Jim said.

Jim's older brother, Gordy, worked at the store from 1949 until he graduated from high school. The next older brother, John, took over managing until his graduation, when he went to Minneapolis where jobs were plentiful compared to Fergus Falls. "Then it was my turn to take over," Jim said.

He has many wonderful memories of the customers served at West End Grocery, although times were tough for many families.

"World War II had ended just a few years earlier in 1945, and it took the economy time to recover," Jim recalled. "Back then, many of our customers just shopped, and we wrote the purchases in a separate book. They paid us on their payday."

One of the highlights for Jim was decorating for Christmas every year, still one of his favorite memories.

"After my dad, Helmer, died in 1962, the store operated until 1965, but then closed after everything became too much for my mother Ruth," he said.

The building still stands, and was at one time used as a pottery school by Jim's sister, Linda. She and her family bought the original home and the store building.

OTHER FOND MEMORIES FROM JIM GERHARDSON

Prior to working at West End Grocery, Jim Gerhardson delivered the *Fergus Falls Daily Journal*.

His route began on North Union Avenue by the old public library, a block north of downtown and up the hill from the old bowling alley. Included were newspaper deliveries along both West Summit Avenue and West Cavour Avenue. He had 160 to 165 papers to deliver six days per week, rain or shine.

Jim delivered to our house, headed by Roy and Claire Hintgen, at 930 West Cavour. My older sister, Catherine, and Jim were classmates in the FFHS Class of 1957, as was classmate Mike Sigelman, who lived right next door to the west of the Hintgen house.

"We were very fortunate kids, all of us, to have lived in Fergus Falls at that time in history," Jim added.

WEST END GROCERY HAD THREE GENERATIONS

Fergus Falls had close to 25 neighborhood grocery stores during the 1950s and 1960s.

West End Grocery at the corner of West Cavour Avenue and Buse Street, also known as Gerhardson's Grocery, was a three-generation enterprise.

Otto Gerhardson started West End Grocery with his wife, Hilma, after their marriage in 1907. They lived down the hill, one house east of Buse Street, facing Lincoln Avenue.

A son, Helmer Otto Gerhardson and his wife, Ruth, then took over the operations of West End Grocery. They lived right next door to the grocery store.

"My Grandma Ruth operated West End Grocery with her 10 children for over a decade, while Grandpa Helmer worked at the State Hospital in Brainerd during the week," said Bob Paulson whose mother, Beverly, was the oldest of the 10 children.

Helmer Otto died at age 54 in 1962 and Ruth continued to operate the grocery store after his death, with her children, until 1965.

"Our family passed along how my great-grandfather, Otto, kept his fiddle at the corner store," said Bob, who with his wife, Cyd, live in Rapid City, South Dakota. "He only played it when his wife, Hilma, wasn't in the store, since fiddling led to dancing."

Bob's mother, Bev, married Lloyd Paulson of Parkers Prairie in 1951 at Augustana Lutheran Church in Fergus Falls.

These days Bob and Cyd spend two months each spring and fall on his great-grandparents' farm west of Parkers Prairie. The family has owned this land since 1892.

Lloyd Paulson was employed by Scheels in Fargo-Moorhead from 1952 to 1980.

"My Mom and Dad were both founding members of the Dollars for Scholars chapters in Parkers Prairie, Fergus Falls and Moorhead," Bob said.

"One of Dad's business associates took Dad's idea and set up Dollars for Scholars chapters in every North Dakota town that had three components: a high school, a newspaper and a bank."

MORE ABOUT WEST END GROCERY

Bob Paulson, great-grandson of West End Grocery founders Otto and Hilma Gerhardson, says his great-grandparents and grandparents sold produce, dairy products, cut meat, lunch meat and sausages to order.

"Kids would return pop bottles daily, often exchanging them for candies in bins behind a tall glass case," he said.

Hunting and fishing stories were shared at a bench in the back of the store, always a source of the latest news.

A buzzer on the front door of the store was wired into the house next door.

"When customers would come by during mealtimes, one of the kids would hustle over to the store to serve the customer," Bob said. "There was a well-trodden path from the side door of the house to the store."

Special orders were either held for customers on any day of the week, or delivered to their homes.

"Put it on our tab" was often requested by customers who were short until the next payday.

DELPHINE SILBERNAGEL'S MEMORIES

Delphine Silbernagel, her older brother, Robbie, and other relatives moved to a house at 705 West Cavour in 1953. Two nephews (Tony and David) and a niece (Kathleen) lived with Delphine and Robbie and attended Our Lady of Victory School, only two blocks to the east past Broadway.

"We were only one house from the end of the street and only had to walk across Buse Street to get to West End Grocery, which we always called Gerhardson's," said Delphine while recalling corner grocery stores in early 2019.

"Mr. Gerhardson died quite young, so Mrs. Gerhardson and the children kept the business going. The kids would ride their bikes and deliver groceries on the west side of town."

"Having this corner grocery store close by was convenient if a person needed a grocery item quickly, an example being when unexpected company arrived," said Delphine who was employed by Northwestern Bell.

"In a few minutes, with Gerhardson's being so close by, we had what was needed to make a meal. Few people had freezers in those days. Everything was made fresh from the market."

During the 1950s and 1960s, the Silbernagels and neighbors on West Cavour especially appreciated this corner grocery store on hot summer days when they could purchase ice cream or cold drinks, "pop" as they called it in those days.

"Our nephews, Tony and David, and niece Kathleen skipped over to Gerhardson's many times a week," Delphine said, "for errands, to buy candy or pop, or to visit with the Gerhardson kids."

One frequent visitor to Gerhardson's Grocery, for candy or pop, was Guy Snoeckx, a foreign exchange student from Belgium. Guy, in 1964-65, lived at the home across the street from the grocery store with Ken and Lillian Hunt and their son, David.

Over the years Delphine Silbernagel frequented many of the 23 grocery stores that were in operation in Fergus Falls in the years following World War II. Four of her brothers served in the military during the war, from 1941 to 1945.

Nesbitt's Orange pop was a hit with kids during the 1950s.

Chapter Twenty-One

Michael Lange Farm in Star Lake Township

by Sharon Voigt Hintgen

LANGE FARM MEMORIES

In the spring of 1910 Michael Lange, my grandfather, moved his family from McLeod County in southern Minnesota to Star Lake Township in Otter Tail County. They were Germans who immigrated to the United States from Prussia in 1888.

Michael, his wife Helen (Herman), and their six children (August Michael, age 14; William Otto, age 12; Ida Augusta, age 9; Erna Mathilda, age 6; Adolph Albert, age 3; and Herman Henry age 3 months) moved to the farm in Star Lake Township.

They purchased a 160-acre farm that included parts of section 29, 30, and 31 for $1,600. They secured a mortgage of $1,200 at 7% interest rate. The farm had some tillable land, along with woods and pasture.

The house was on the farm, and probably the barn also. There was also a granary and chicken coop.

They had five additional children born on the farm. Helen Alice Louise was the first, born on January 5, 1912. Next came Ella Hattie, born April 29, 1914, followed by Elwin

Harry, November 29, 1916, Maynard Arnold, June 25, 1914, and finally my mother, Delores Mae on July 11, 1923. All the children were born in the house without a doctor. A doctor was called for Delores, but she was born before he arrived.

They were neighbors to the Henry and Emma Koellen farm, another German family who had previously lived in southern Minnesota. They had a feuding relationship and each ended up with their own line fence between their farms.

Life on the farm centered around the family, the farm animals and the chores. Music, playing cards and visiting neighbors and family was their main social life.

Michael made home brew beer and also enjoyed going to the saloons in Dent. He loved the horses the most of all the animals. It was a typical small diversified farm with some wheat, corn, oats and hay. Some of the wheat and corn would be sold to pay the mortgage interest. Milk and beef were most

Lange Barn in Star Lake Township

likely sold to the Creamery in Dent. The sheep wool was sold, as well as lambs. Some of the milk, pigs and beef cattle were also sold.

The family used the milk, beef, pigs, chickens, turkeys, ducks and geese for food. Of course, they always had a dog to help bring home the dairy cows and cats to take care of the vermin in the barn. They also had a large vegetable garden to provide fresh vegetables during the summer and canned vegetables during the winter.

Music was a large part of the family's entertainment. All of the children were musical and most played a musical instrument. Adolph, Ella, Helen and Delores all played the piano. Ida played the harmonica and Maynard the guitar. William, Elwin and August played the violin. Herman liked to sing and he sang. Their mother, Helen, played the concertina.

The family played lots of card games, such as Rummy. There was always a houseful of people with family and friends. This was especially true on Sunday afternoons.

Helen, the mother, did most of the cooking. The kids said she could make tasty food out of meager rations. She always made enough to feed her large family. She made several loaves of bread every other day. She mixed the dough in a large crock bowl and baked it in a wood-fired cookstove. She made the food while the older girls like Helen and Ella took care of the younger children Maynard and Delores.

The Langes made and ate the typical German fare such as sauerkraut, chocolate soup (soup made from duck blood), head cheese, blood sausage and other sausages. They smoked ham and bacon, and made their own soap from rendered lard.

The school-age children walked to Zorn School District 137 (rural School District 137). During the 1930s Depression years, many times they only had lard or syrup bread in their lunch pail.

In July of 1936, during a hot, dry day, Michael died. He was 75 years old. He was buried at Silent Vale Cemetery near the Maine Presbyterian Church.

Elwin and Maynard worked at the Civilian Conservation Corps (CCC) camps before World War II to help support the family.

Lange Family
Back, l-r: Helen, Michael, Erna Lange Freeman, baby Michael Freeman,
Helen Lange Freeman and Ella Lange
Front, l-r: Maynard Lange, Delores Lange, Mervin Freeman and
Darlene Freeman

There are many stories from the farm. Delores was cleaning the sheep pen when she turned her back on the ram and he got her in the butt. She hit him with the pitch fork and never turned her back on him again. She said that if he came at you all you had to do was step to the side and he would go by as he had so much wool around his eyes he had no peripheral vision.

The Langes had a Hereford bull they called Ferdinand, which Delores said was so gentle she could get on his back and he would walk around if she twisted his tail.

Delores loved the work horses and would ride them bareback to get the cows in for milking. She used to drive a team of horses to cultivate the corn and do other chores.

Delores liked to work outside with Herman on the farm. Helen, Herman and Delores were the last to live on the farm. Delores married Irvin Voigt and left the farm in 1947, and Helen died in 1949. Delores always longed for the farm. Herman took over the farm and married Lila Field. Later it was sold to Leigh Field.

Maynard was known as the trickster of the family. Emma Koellen didn't want him to cut across their land on the way to and from school. He once shot her bloomers hanging on the clothes line with his shotgun.

In the summer, the family would cut down trees in the woods and make a huge wood pile for the winter. They also cut ice from the lake and stored it in straw for use in the summer ice box. The winters could be long, and chores always had to be done. During a snowstorm they would attach a rope from the house to the barn so they wouldn't get lost or disoriented.

They didn't have running water, but had a small pump in the kitchen and large pump outside by the barn to fill the water tanks for the animals.

In the fall, the boys would hunt ducks, pheasants and deer. In the summer, they would fish. They did swim in Star Lake, but there was not much time to go to the lake.

During World War II, gas and sugar were rationed. Meat and some food items were also rationed, but they raised those on the farm so it did not affect them.

Summer entertainment revolved around the local baseball team. Adolph, Herman, Elwin and Maynard all played on the Star Lake Team. Sundays were for church, family dinners and visiting with family and friends.

Chapter Twenty-Two

My Aunt Ella's Farm

by Sharon Voigt Hintgen

SHARON'S MEMORIES

As kids we always loved to go out to Aunt Ella's farm. Actually, it was my Aunt Ella and Clifford Veazie's farm in Star Lake Township. Clifford developed multiple sclerosis when quite young, so he was housebound most of the time I knew him.

Ella was my mother's closest sister as she was nine years older and practically raised my mother, Delores Lange Voigt. Their mother was busy cooking and taking care of a large farm family, so Ella and her sister Helen were responsible for the youngest siblings.

Ella's farm was 150 acres bordering one of many Mud Lakes in Star Lake Township. There were woods, pasture and some tillable land. Clifford and Ella bought the farm in 1938.

It was a small diversified farm that had chickens, some milk cows, ducks, dogs and cats. They had two sons, Warren and Mike.

When Clifford first farmed, he had horses. The team Mike remembers is Dick and Dolly.

Aerial photo of Aunt Ella's farm

The original home was a small, two-story house with a narrow, steep stairs going up to the bedrooms. It had a root cellar that had a door on the floor.

Later on, family and friends built a downstairs bedroom, bathroom and living room, with a full basement underneath.

My cousin Warren built trails in the woods. We had a gold mine, trees laying down to jump over and some to climb. As kids we had a turned-over wooden wagon box that we used as a house with some furniture and household items.

In the summer, my brothers Tom and Richard, my cousin Mike and I would run through the woods. We would play in the woods until we would come in for lunch. My Aunt Ella was a wonderful cook and she always had sandwiches with homemade buns, and lots of sweets.

Aunt Ella made cakes from scratch and wonderful buttermilk donuts. She had a large garden and made wonderful dill pickles. Ella had canned stewing hens she would use to make sandwiches. She always served us on her blue willow dishes.

Sometimes I would go with my aunt to feed the calves. I remember that my aunt had to help hold the pail, as the calves drank so fast and butted hard against the pail so I could hardly hold on.

Other times we would gather eggs in the chicken coop and play with the new kittens in the barn. Ella also had baby bantam chicks, and sometimes ducks and ducklings.

There was a creek just over the hill. We would go down and watch the fish run, or throw sticks and watch them go in the culvert under the road and come out the other side. Sometimes we speared suckers and bullheads in the creek.

There also was an old metal spring chained between two large trees that worked as a swing, along with a tire swing on an old oak.

Sometimes we kids got into trouble. My brother Richard and cousin Mike were the same age. One day when they were young, they decided to collect the eggs in the chicken coop. They had about 8-10 eggs and then they threw them against the barn. I don't know if Richard got into trouble, but Mike remembers getting yelled at for the prank.

Aunt Ella always had a dog and it usually loved to fetch. We would throw a tennis ball and the dog would fetch. I remember that Ben, an old black lab, would never stop. Dad said we had to give him a rest as he would never stop running as long as we would throw the ball. On a hot day he could get overheated.

When the weather was too cold to play outside, we would play in the hay loft of the barn. Of course, everyone had the square bales then. They weren't really square, but rectangular and they were great for constructing forts. My cousins had constructed forts and they would be connected all under the bales with tunnels. It was nice and warm and we would come into the house with our clothes and hair full of hay.

One winter, my Uncle Clifford didn't realize that there was not nearly as much hay as he thought. We had used so much of the hay loft with forts and tunnels and he was forced to buy hay for the cattle.

Ella had a two-seater outhouse that the family used for many years before they had running water. We thought it was fun to use the outhouse.

My Aunt Ella was such a nice person and she always had things for us to do. She belonged to two Ladies Aid groups and was well liked. She was very active in the Maine Presbyterian Church and Camp Joy.

People would stop by and visit when we were at Aunt Ella's farm. We loved going there. When we were playing outside, my mother and Ella were inside. They would play hymns on the piano and harmonize. Sometimes all of the adults would play whist.

l-r: Randa Veazie (Clifford's mother), Clifford and Ella Veazie, Tom and Richard Voigt, and Michael Veazie

Chapter Twenty-Three

Broadway Market

Diann Hennig's Memories

Fergus Falls, following World War II from the late 1940s to the 1970s, had 23 neighborhood grocery stores.

One of those stores is fondly recalled by Diann Hennig, FFHS class of 1960, whose parents ran Broadway Market on the 800 block of North Broadway.

"My first recollections of Broadway Market go back to when my parents, Vern and Hilda Hennig, bought the store about 1948," Diann said.

She was in the first grade at McKinley School and her older sister, Sidonna (now Sidonna Bradow), was in third grade.

"My parents moved back to Fergus after having spent several years in the 1930s and 1940s in Detroit, Michigan, where my dad was a milkman," she said. "On his first route he used a horse-drawn cart."

Vern and Hilda had both grown up in and near Fergus Falls, and they returned after the war to purchase the store on North Broadway.

Hilda and Vern Hennig, operators of Broadway Market in Fergus Falls

"My grandma and grandpa, Bill and Gustie Hennig, had purchased a house on Broadway, and we lived there until my parents bought the store," Diann recalls.

"Dad and mom began expanding things soon after they purchased the store," she said. "For a number of years, Broadway Market was also our home. Dad and mom put an addition onto the store building and we lived there for several years."

Work and home life were totally knitted together, and when Diann and her sister were old enough they worked in the store.

"When our parents did take a vacation, Sidonna and I would run the store with help from Hazel Evenson, a neighbor across the street," Diann said. "Living in the store had its advantages. The delicious aroma from our home-cooked meals probably helped stimulate sales."

In 1955, Vern and Hilda built a house across the street from the store, and then expanded Broadway Market into the area in which they had been living, except for the bathroom and kitchen.

Vern, although having little education, was blessed with a real knack for sales. Hilda did all of the bookkeeping.

Diann remembers her father as a funny and gregarious guy who loved to argue, often just for the sake of arguing.

"Some of our customers loved to come in just to talk and argue with him," recalls Diann.

She and her sister, Sidonna, were expected to work in the store. They put in lots of hours until they graduated from high school and began their own lives.

"The store was a way of life," Diann says. "We were open from 7 a.m. to 10 p.m., seven days a week, and were kind of a mini supermarket. We were closed from 1 p.m. to 3 p.m. on Christmas Day so we could have Christmas dinner. That was literally our only holiday."

The Broadway Market phone number was 6666, and then later Regent 6-6666.

"At one point, Phillips 66 wanted to buy our number, but my dad refused," Diann said. "My sister and I stayed off the phone because we took phone orders and made home deliveries long before the era of real supermarkets."

Diann and Sidonna made some of the deliveries.

"My dad made me start driving when I was 15 so I could deliver groceries or beer or whatever a customer needed," Diann said. "I drove a great '42 Chevy."

Her father would buy sides of beef and do the butchering right in the kitchen. Vern made his own sausage, and sliced lunch meats. He also bought chickens and eggs from local farmers.

Vern and Hilda sold Broadway Market in the early 1960s. Vern worked briefly as a salesman at the Montgomery Ward's store on East Lincoln in Fergus Falls. He and Hilda then moved to the Twin Cities, where Vern worked at SuperValu in Richfield.

Diann, who currently lives in Minnetonka near the Twin Cities, worked over the years doing jobs ranging from secretarial work to selling apples to being a rural mail carrier to teaching water aerobics.

"I never had anyone harder to work for than my dad," she said. "He and the Broadway Market really gave me a work ethic that has stuck with me for my entire life."

MORE RECOLLECTIONS OF BROADWAY MARKET

"We didn't have air conditioning, and in the summer we sold lots of ice cream in cones and in bulk," said Diann. "A single scoop was a nickel and a double was a dime."

She said Broadway Market stocked a lot of candy, all kept under a glass case.

"Occasionally, kids would try to steal and I would sometimes have to chase them down. We were very popular on Halloween because dad would give out 5-cent candy bars."

Broadway Market allowed people to charge for their groceries.

"But sometimes they wouldn't pay," Diann recalls. "As a last resort, my grandma would do the collecting. But when people paid their bills, my dad would toss in a pint of ice cream. "

It was sometimes Diann's job to take money to the bank.

"I would just get on my bicycle with a big wad of cash and head for the bank," she said.

Chapter Twenty-Four

Beck Twins, East Alcott

CAROLYN BECK GLESNE'S MEMORIES

Linwood and Joycelyn Beck raised four sons at 532 East Alcott Avenue in Fergus Falls. Linwood operated Fergus Hatchery.

They raised twins Chuck and Dick, along with Dan and Tom, across from Grotto Lake.

Carolyn Beck Glesne, daughter of Charles and Joyce Beck, said older cousins Chuck and Dick always took time to spend with their younger cousins.

"Cherished memories include skating on Grotto Lake, right across the street from the Linwood Beck home," Carolyn said, "and swimming at Wall Lake during family reunions."

CHUCK BECK WAS A QUIET LEADER

The passing of 1963 Fergus Falls High School graduate Chuck Beck on May 23, 2020, in Bend, Oregon, led to several accolades from his classmates and relatives.

"Chuck and his twin brother, Dick, were quiet leaders – both in the classroom and on the athletic field," said fellow 1963 FFHS grad Steve Emerson. "As individuals, they had a good sibling rivalry."

The Beck twins, who later became physicians, participated in football, basketball, track, band and other activities at Fergus Falls High School.

The Fergus Falls Otter 880-yard (half-mile) relay team took fourth place at the state track meet in the spring of 1963.
l-r: Larry Rose, Chuck Beck, Dave Olson and Dick Beck
Photo courtesy of Dick Beck

"They were well rounded individuals," Emerson said. "Chuck and Dick had a reputation for excelling in each of the activities in which they pursued."

Kids around town came to know the Beck twins in the 1950s through the grade school basketball program.

"Many of us couldn't tell them apart," Emerson said, "and even the coach had to rely on them having different colored socks for identification purposes."

Ken Kothe, another 1963 FFHS grad, also praises Chuck and Dick Beck.

"Chuck was our senior year quarterback and had great leadership," Kothe said. "Head coach Rocky Elton also appreciated Chuck's leadership."

The Beck family welcomed players into their home for visits, and even overnight stays. While Chuck Beck played quarterback, brother Dick was a running back.

The Beck twins also were teammates of Kothe on the Otter varsity basketball squad. In the spring Kothe played baseball, while the Beck twins participated in track.

Kothe, Chuck and Dick Beck were among the active and honorary pallbearers for the 1970 funeral of classmate Mike Jenson, who died in Vietnam while serving his country.

Chuck was named after his father's brother, artist Charles Beck who later taught art at M State, Fergus Falls. Dick was named after his mother's brother, Richard Utne.

The Beck twins ran the snack bar adjacent to the changing rooms at Pebble Lake in the summer of 1962. Pop sold for 10 cents and candy also sold for a dime.

Back then, a walkway took swimmers to the snack bar and changing rooms on the east side of the waterfront, below the hill where kids would frolic.

Their boss was summer recreation director Oats LeGrand. They also were pole vaulters for LeGrand's Otter varsity track team.

"One spring we had an indoor track meet in Grand Forks," Dick Beck recalls. "Oats drove his light aqua Ford station wagon with our aluminum vaulting pole strapped to the door handles."

LeGrand lit a cigar.

"The distance between Fergus and Grand Forks equaled the life of his cigar," Dick said.

"Our dear Grandma Nellie Beck faithfully listened to Oats LeGrand's Otter sports radio broadcasts," Carolyn said. "We remember more than once being with her during a broadcast."

If the score was close with seconds left in the game and they heard, "Beck has the ball," Grandma Nellie would turn off the radio, too nervous to listen.

"We would turn it back on when the game was over to see what happened," Carolyn said.

The Beck cousins were always eager to listen to Chuck's medical school stories when he was at the University of Minnesota, especially his experiences at Hennepin County General Hospital.

Chuck Beck loved the outdoors.

"We never tired of hearing about his latest mountain trek, bicycling adventure or prized catch in a trout stream," Carolyn said. "He was a warm, thoughtful and genuine person. We will truly miss the twinkle of humor in his eyes and his kind heart."

MORE FROM DICK BECK

Fergus Falls High School 1963 graduate Dick Beck and his late brother, Chuck Beck, had many wonderful memories of their growing up years in Fergus Falls.

"We started pole vaulting in our garden behind the house at 532 E Alcott. We used a bamboo pole and bamboo cross bar," Dick said. "The standards were makeshift, and we cleared 6-7 feet."

By the time they were high school seniors, with the aluminum pole, their pole vaulting height had increased to about 11 feet 6 inches.

"Another project, as kids, was building non-motorized go carts," Dick recalls. "They were 5-foot, 2-inch x 12-inch and equipped with steering and brakes made from broom handles and rope."

The brake was a board on the side. When raised it compressed the back wheel. Their track was Arlington Avenue from Alcott down to Vernon Avenue.

"As seniors, Chuck and I wore new all-leather football helmets with good interior padding."

In the fall of 1962, Chuck suffered a season-ending head and neck injury in the third game of their senior season at Detroit Lakes.

"We were 3-0 up to that point and lost the rest of the games. However, the competition also was tougher."

Dick says that he and Chuck always enjoyed a healthy academic competition, especially as roommates at the University of Minnesota, followed by Medical School at the U of M.

Chapter Twenty-Five

Ken Kothe from Elizabeth

KEN'S MEMORIES

Ken remembers a slightly chilly yet sunny day in early September 1960, when he and his father, older brother Richard, older sister Connie and younger brother Edward met with Principal Ed Bechtel to enroll at Fergus Falls High School. His father, the Rev. Herbert Kothe, had just accepted a call as pastor of St John's Lutheran Church in Elizabeth.

Ken Kothe, a 1963 graduate of Fergus Falls High School, fondly recalls his participation in Otter athletics – in 1962-63, he was Otter MVP in football, basketball and baseball.

"There were 12 children in our immediate family, six boys and six girls, and my Mom (Martha) took care of all us. By the time we moved to Elizabeth, there were just four of us in school. She was a wonderful mother and a saint in our eyes."

At first, Ken says their move from Fairhaven, Minnesota, south of St. Cloud, was emotionally difficult. "We all had feelings of loneliness and missing our friends."

However, the Kothe siblings quickly made new friends in Elizabeth and Fergus Falls.

"It was sports for my brothers and me, and cheerleading for Connie," Ken says.

Richard Kothe graduated from FFHS in 1961, Connie in 1962, Ken in 1963 and Ed in 1964.

"I remember quite a few cold, wintry mornings walking by St. John's, jogging over Highway 59 and passing by the telephone booth to the only grocery store/post office in Elizabeth, waiting for the school bus to pick us up," Ken recalls.

Once in the store, he saw several students with the names Fick, Thompson and Nelson, and a variety of Wildes.

"But what caught my eye most were four tall men and one short burly man," Ken says. "Charlie, Jim and Tom Blondeau and Tom Prischmann were the four tall guys. Carl Prischmann was the short and burly one, who was an excellent baseball player."

To this day he believes that he and his brother Richard must have also stood out that day.

"We were the only ones wearing black (Wyatt Earp) overcoats and (Elliot Ness) fedora hats, popular among people in those days," Ken said. "Edward also wore a fedora, but a gray overcoat. Richard and I thought that he was not quite ready for a 'prime time' Wyatt Earp overcoat."

Ken says he will always remember the summer of 1961, when he flipped hamburgers for Bert Skogmo at Dairyland on North Union Avenue in Fergus Falls.

"Bert was focused and definitely was a tasked-oriented person," Ken says, "but he was always good to me. He would let me off work early to play Fergus Falls American Legion baseball, coached by Harley Oyloe."

He is like many former players who praise Oyloe as a great baseball coach in Fergus Falls.

"Bert enjoyed playing catch before letting me leave Dairyland to play a Legion baseball game," Ken recalls. "I enjoyed it, too."

"That year, 1961, we made it back to the state Legion baseball tournament, after winning the state title in 1960. This time, however, we lost to eventual state champion, St. Paul Christi de Parc. Some great memories."

Ken, at Fergus Falls High School, was named MVP in football, basketball and baseball his senior year, in 1962-63.

He is married to 1964 FFHS graduate Katherine Beamish. Together, they are proud of their four children and grandchildren. Ken, like his father, went into the ministry. Katherine became a nurse.

KOTHE REMEMBERS JENSON, HENSCH

In 2020, Ken Kothe recalled 1963 FFHS classmate Mike Jenson, who died 50 years previously during the Vietnam War. The exact date of Mike's death was May 9, 1970.

"After graduating from Fergus Falls Junior College (now M State), Mike and I enrolled at Moorhead State College and roomed together in a dormitory" Kothe said.

"Later on, in the fall of 1966, Richard Hensch (FFHS class of 1964) moved in with us off campus."

Hensch later became a career Navy pilot.

During his 22-year military service, Hensch had the honor to fly the A-4 Skyhawk and the A-7 Corsair II, and had nearly 500 aircraft carrier landings. He died on March 21, 2020.

Kothe, an Army veteran, remembers one afternoon when Mike walked into their apartment and with great delight said he just bought two tickets for a concert on campus.

Performing was the singing group, Jay and the Americans.

Something else came up and Kothe had to turn down Jenson's invitation to attend the concert, even though Kothe enjoyed Jay and the Americans' music.

"Who Mike went with I can't recall," Kothe said. "When he returned that night, he was very excited and happy."

That fall Jenson signed up for a class on dancing.

"Neither one of us danced very well," Kothe said, "but after a few classes Mike showed me what he had learned."

It was a dance popular in those days, one that Mike Love of The Beach Boys performed during some of their music concerts.

"As a dancer, Mike became smooth and graceful," Kothe said. "Even at that time I admired him and wished I could dance like him."

FFHS basketball player Ken Kothe in the middle of the action against the Detroit Lakes Lakers

13 STRAIGHT FREE THROWS

Ken Kothe remembers a basketball game at Alexandria his senior year, in 1963. It was the last game of the season before subdistricts and it was very strange.

Kothe, during his induction into the Fergus Falls Chamber of Commerce Sports Hall of Fame on Aug. 11, 2018, quoted Mark Twain as an introduction to three stories he wanted to tell.

"I told two and forget the most unusual one of all," he said. From Mark Twain:

*When I was younger I could remember anything, whether it had happened or not; but my faculties are decaying now, and soon I shall be so I cannot remember any but the things that **never** happened.*

Kothe recalls that when he was younger his memory was very good in some areas.

"I would calculate my baseball batting average, in my mind, after every time at bat, and counted points in basketball as the game was going on. I'm older now, but still remember one very unusual happening."

He continues, "My family tells me I now remember 'things that never happened', but this is not the case regarding the game in 1963. Those things back then really did happen."

In February 1963, the Otter boys basketball team played the Cardinals in Alexandria.

Dick Seal was the *Daily Journal*'s sports editor at the time and covered the game, which is in the *Daily Journal* archives.

"His reporting was accurate, as far as it goes, but it doesn't go far enough," Ken says. "After all, how could Dick know and report on what he did not see? So for him and others it would seem that nothing of significance happened. But it did, and I remember it very well."

Offensively and defensively, Kothe sought to be around the basketball as much as possible.

"I remember the very first foul of the game. The referee grabbed me out of the scuffle and marched me to the free throw lane. I missed both free throws."

He said that missing those free throws drove him, all the more, to intercept a pass, to force a turnover or to draw a foul.

"And in doing so I tussled with the Alexandria players as they (the Cardinals) fouled other Fergus Otters. Those other Otters never shot their free throws."

The question became, "Well, who did?"

The other Otters, Dan Larson, Bobby Warn and Harold Tysver may have been the ones fouled. But Kothe quickly separated from the scuffle, walked directly to the free throw lane, and shot their free throws.

Kothe says that maybe it was Dick Beck, Charles Beck or Steve Emerson who were robbed of their free throws. Or it might have been Roger Fleming, Dave Anderson, Wayne Sandberg, Bruce Josephs or Chuck Christopherson.

"I still to this day don't know," Kothe says.

"Not even Coach Ken Naffziger nor Assistant Coach John Hermès appeared to know. If they did, they said nothing about it. In any case, I shot other Otters' free throws. I made 13 straight that night, and 14 would have been a record in 1963."

The fact that Dick Seal and others knew nothing about it then does not surprise Kothe.

Years later, in 2005, Kothe joined in celebrating the life of Carla Warn Lehtinen, a classmate and dear friend, in Bloomington, Minnesota.

"I mentioned this 1963 basketball game story to Bobby Warn and Dan Larson," Ken says, "and they vaguely remembered the night of my free throws."

Like Twain said, "When I was younger I could remember anything, whether it had happened or not; but my faculties are decaying now, and soon I shall be so I cannot remember any but the things that **never** happened."

Chapter Twenty-Six

Piekarski Farm Memories

PIEKARSKI MEMORIES

Charles Piekarski, with his wife, Carol, have farmed in Carlisle Township, northwest of Fergus Falls, from 1972 through 2021.

Back in 1973, Charles and his father, Steve, were featured in the *Fergus Falls Daily Journal*.

Newspaper staff writer Bill Bank noted that at that time, 48 years ago, soybean prices were high. That was due, in part, to a lifting of an embargo on soybean exports along with severe flooding of crops down south in the Mississippi Valley.

Daily Journal chief photographer Harley Oyloe took a photo of Charles operating a cultivator and Steve running a combine.

In 1973, Charles and Steve Piekarski were about to benefit, as were other area farmers, from an increase of 33 million bushels of soybeans to overseas markets. That year there was not enough soybeans to meet the overseas demand.

Steve Piekarski told the *Daily Journal* that soybeans "aren't any harder to cultivate than corn and some other crops. However, soybeans require quite a bit more moisture for the beans to come around right."

He and Charles added that soybeans were quite susceptible to hail and wind damage but they could withstand drought almost as well as corn.

Steve served as an Army Air Force flight engineer and gunner for four years during World War II. He married Rachel Sanco at Our Lady of Victory Church, Fergus Falls, in 1946. They had three sons, Charles, John and James.

Steve and Rachel lived and farmed in Carlisle Township until 1978 when they moved to Long Lake. Rachel died in January 1996 and Steve died in August 2005.

Steve Piekarski with combine on his 640-acre farm in Carlisle Township in 1973. The self-propelled 12-foot combine did its job after the grain was cut by a swather. Photo courtesy of Fergus Falls Daily Journal

Charles Piekarski on the farm in 1973.
He performed field work with use of a cultivator.
Photo courtesy of Fergus Falls Daily Journal

Charles Piekarski, with his wife, Carol, have enjoyed farming from 1972 through this year.

Brother John and his wife, Sandy, farm at an adjoining farm in Carlisle Township. Brother James and his wife, Sharon, who live in Detroit Lakes, own a portion of the Piekarski farmsteads.

James helps Charles with farm work as does Steve Roehl, a classmate of Charles. Both graduated from Fergus Falls High School in 1966.

Crops in previous years have been wheat and barley. In recent years the main crops on the Piekarski farms have been corn and soybeans. John provides seeds for various companies.

The late Steve Piekarski's brother, Leonard Piekarski, and his wife, Darlene, also farmed in Carlisle Township. They had three sons, Pete, Tom and Jonathan and a daughter, Cleo. Steve and Leonard had six siblings.

Chapter Twenty-Seven

Old Baseball Park

OLD BALLPARK MEMORIES

In the 1950s and 1960s, Fergus Falls home baseball games took place at a ballpark west of the high school football field and north of what was then the old fairgrounds. This was prior to construction of the new middle school, starting in 1967 and following the fire that destroyed Washington Junior High.

The old fairgrounds is now the location for Kennedy Secondary School, upgraded from the former middle school. The old senior high now houses community education, the special education cooperative and offices.

The site of the old baseball field in Fergus Falls is now a playground, located north of Kennedy Secondary School for students in grades 5 through 12. Baseball games now are played at the American Legion field at DeLagoon Park, north of Pebble Lake.

This old ballpark near Friberg Avenue was, in fact, at one time a neighborhood baseball park in Fergus Falls.

It was a similar situation as Wrigley Field, home of the Chicago Cubs, in a neighborhood on the north side of Chicago.

The old baseball park in Fergus Falls was located just west of the high school football field. Today the land is used as a playground just north of Kennedy School. The playground equipment shown in photo is located at what was once the infield at the old ballpark.

The grandstands behind home plate, used for baseball games, were also used during the county fair. Traveling shows entertained fairgoers with acts that included dog shows, tumbling, low-wire acts, ventriloquists, comedians, musicians and others.

The western section was an old wooden grandstand, and a modern cement-block grandstand comprised the eastern section. During baseball games there also were bleachers on the first base and third base sides.

The old Fergus Falls ballpark scoreboard was situated behind the left field fence. The entire outfield fence, from left to right, was painted with various advertisements.

Long-time Fergus Falls residents remember the stock car racing track that ran between home plate and the grandstands.

"That made for a long distance behind home plate to the grandstand," Mark Oyloe said. "If a ball got past the catcher, he had a long ways to chase it. It also was a long ways for the catcher to run and catch pop ups."

During the 1950s and 1960s, lights at the Fergus baseball park on North Friberg Avenue would attract fans to town baseball games, American Legion baseball games and VFW baseball games.

As fans got closer to the park, there would be the aroma of popcorn and hot dogs that were for sale. It was a fun neighborhood atmosphere.

"During the early 1950s, people stayed closer to home and attended many of our Fergus Red Sox games," said retiree Harley Oyloe. "One year we averaged close to 1,300 people at each home game."

In those days television was just taking hold, many area roads were gravel, and cars had lots of flat tires and overheated radiators.

Oyloe very well remembers the third base bleachers.

"That's where Sonny Mjelde, Norm Galloway and some of the other characters sat. Sonny could be easily heard from there. He particularly liked to heckle the Willmar manager when he coached near third base."

The year 1960 was the last of 15 years referred to by many as the golden era of Minnesota amateur baseball, covering the years from 1946 to 1960, following World War II. The book, *Town Ball*, covers those glory days. There's lots of information about Fergus Falls baseball in the book.

The 1950 Fergus Falls Red Sox were state champions, defeating Austin 3-0 in the title game at St. Cloud. Oyloe was the winning pitcher for Fergus Falls. Red Sox reunions were held in 1970 and 1992.

The summer of 1960 was the final year for the Minneapolis Millers minor league team. In 1961, the Minnesota Twins commenced play at Metropolitan Stadium in Bloomington.

In 1960, the Fergus Falls VFW baseball team, coached by Oats LeGrand, and the American Legion baseball team, coached by Oyloe, won state titles. The town team Red Sox took second at the State Class B baseball tournament. The Fergus Falls player-manager was Roland Harlow.

A combined 50th reunion for all three Fergus Falls baseball teams from 1960 was held July 10, 2010, at the Fergus Falls American Legion.

FERGUS RED SOX GLORY YEAR RECALLED

Downtown businessman Bob Allison, in May 1950, was president of the board of directors for the Fergus Falls Red Sox town baseball team. He was highly optimistic at the start of the season. Agreeing with that optimism were the other Red Sox board members, who included George Wagner, Knute Hanson, Howard Sowden, Harold Mittelstadt, Wally Holmquist, Dick Raiter, Bud Christenson, Bill Nelson, Ben Wyffels and Dick McAlpin.

In those days, players were lured to Fergus Falls from other states to join with team members raised in Minnesota.

The only Fergus Falls players on the 1950 Red Sox team were Harley Oyloe and Roland Harlow.

The players who came from out of town, and from different areas of the United States, worked part-time for Fergus Falls businesses, the city park department and other employers, in addition to playing baseball for the town team Red Sox.

Home games were played at the old fairgrounds baseball field, just north of what today is Kennedy Secondary School.

After four years of hard work, Red Sox club finances for 1950 were in good shape.

"We have a well-balanced team this year," said Allison, who had the same name as future Minnesota Twins player Bob Allison.

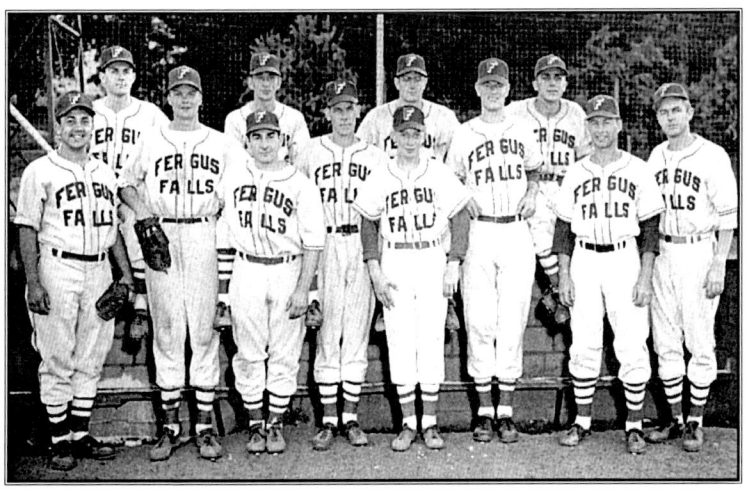

The 1950 state champion Fergus Falls Red Sox
Front, l-r: Jim McNulty, Don Blasius, Ed Piacentini, John Kelly, George Sawyer (batboy), John DeWitt, Hal Younghans, and Harley Oyloe.
Back, l-r: Fred Kroog, Rollie Harlow, Duane Baglien and Joe Colasinski.
Photo courtesy of Town Ball *baseball book editors.*

All of this optimism came to fruition when, in September 1950, the Fergus Falls Red Sox won the Class AA state title over Austin, 3-0, at Municipal Stadium in St. Cloud.

Oyloe pitched the shutout for Fergus Falls in the championship game. He twice struck out Austin star and future New York Yankee Bill "Moose" Skowron.

A victory parade was held in downtown Fergus Falls. Player-manager Jim McNulty, at the conclusion of the parade, presented the state tournament championship trophy to board president Allison.

Oyloe, 10 years later, coached the Fergus Falls American Legion team to the state title.

MORE RED SOX MEMORIES

Dayton Soby, a member of the Fergus Falls High School Class of 1957, remembers the 1950 Fergus Red Sox team members.

"I was 11 at the time," he says. "First baseman Don Blasius stayed in a bedroom in my parents' house that summer. I recall going fishing on Long Lake, on a pontoon, with Blasius and others."

Happy to host Blasius in their home were B.K. Soby and his wife, Lucile.

Third baseman Ed Piacentini also stayed at the Soby home for a short while, and then stayed at the home of Ed and Adeline Karst.

Blasius and Piacentini both came to the Fergus Falls Red Sox from Northwestern University in Evanston, Illinois.

They blended well with local team members, who included pitcher Harley Oyloe, a Fergus Falls photographer, and right fielder Roland Harlow, who worked for the Fergus Falls Public Schools system.

Dayton Soby, now a resident of rural Brainerd, vividly remembers the victory parade in downtown Fergus Falls after the Red Sox won the Class AA title in St. Cloud.

"It was really special getting autographs from the players after the parade," he said.

In 1950, the Red Sox won 50 games and lost only 6 times during the championship year. During the season, the Red Sox played 31 games at home.

Home attendance averaged close to 1,000 fans in the late 1940s and early 1950s in Fergus Falls. Many fans, among them corner grocery store owner Sonny Mjelde and milkman LeRoy Quernemoen, rarely missed home games.

Many Red Sox games didn't start until 8 p.m., allowing time for farmers to milk their cows and still drive to Fergus Falls to see most of the action. Banners were strung along Lincoln Avenue buildings in downtown, with the words "Baseball Tonight."

OYLOE HAS FOND BASEBALL MEMORIES

Centenarian Harley Oyloe, in 2021, recalled the many players who came to Fergus Falls from around the United States to play for the town team Red Sox in the late 1940s and early 1950s. They not only were great athletes, but also were gifted individuals who had fulfilling careers.

Oyloe and Roland Harlow were the only players from Fergus Falls who were members of the town team Red Sox, winners of the state Class AA baseball title in 1950.

Jim McNulty, second baseman and Red Sox player-manager in 1950, had formerly played in the Brooklyn Dodgers organization.

"Jim was a former Marine from World War II who served during the Battle of Iwo Jima," said Oyloe, also a military veteran.

McNulty worked the summer of 1950 in Fergus Falls as a part-time employee of the city water and light department, along with playing baseball for the local town team. Other players also had part-time jobs during the summer months.

The caliber of baseball that was played in Fergus Falls during the semi-pro era was amazing. Many of the players were former pros. Others went on to play in the majors after they played for some of the Minnesota teams.

The semi-pro town teams played exhibition games against Northern League teams and beat them regularly.

Playing in Fergus Falls for the Red Sox in 1952 was first baseman Don Herman, son of major league baseball star Babe Herman.

In those days, the home baseball infield was located near what today is playground equipment north of Kennedy School and close to Friberg Avenue. The present-day school site, in the 1950s and 1960s, was the location of the West Otter Tail County fairgrounds.

"Don Herman later on lured his father, Babe, into growing orchids," Oyloe said.

This pursuit led to a business called, "the Orchid Society of Southern California." The father-son team developed award-winning orchids labeled "Rajah's Ruby" and "Babe's Baby."

"Don later traveled to Japan as part of their award-winning orchid business," Oyloe added.

In 1953, former major league pitcher Johnny Gee came to Fergus Falls to pitch for the town team Red Sox. He stood 6 feet 9 inches and was the tallest pitcher to ever play in the big leagues until Randy Johnson debuted for the Montreal Expos in 1988. Johnson was referred to as "The Big Unit."

Rudy Regalado was a member of the Fergus Falls Red Sox in 1952, played minor league baseball for the Cleveland Indians in 1953, and made it to the major leagues in 1954, playing for Cleveland in the World Series. Regalado had played shortstop for the Fergus Falls Red Sox.

"Our 1950 third baseman, Ed Piacentini, a member of our Red Sox state title team, used a different last name, Bernardi, for business purposes," Oyloe said.

Bernardi is credited with writing two novels. His first book, *The Reluctant Patriot: An Italian Tragedy*, chronicles the courage of individuals during World War II and during what he terms "the vendetta peace" in Italy that followed. *Kill the Devil Twice: An Italian Memoir* is the sequel to his first book.

Oyloe and Piacentini are the only members of the 1950 Red Sox state title squad still with us.

Dick Durrell, the founder of *People Magazine* for Time-Life® in the 1970s, played summer baseball in the late 1940s for the Fergus Falls Red Sox town team.

John DeWitt, Red Sox left fielder in 1950, enjoyed his college life at Texas A&M University, where he led the Southwest Conference in home runs in the spring of 1949.

The late 1940s and early 1950s were a time when the Kansas City Monarchs, a traveling African American team, barnstormed through the Upper Midwest. One of their stops was in Fergus Falls.

Those years are referred to by many people as "the golden era of town baseball in Minnesota."

CARMEN COZZA REMEMBERED

The passing of retired Yale head football coach Carmen Cozza in 2018 caught the attention of people who remember Cozza playing town baseball in Fergus Falls.

Cozza was an Ohio native who played part of the 1953 season for the Cleveland Indians minor league team, the Superior Blues, finishing the summer as a pitcher and outfielder with the Fergus Falls Red Sox.

Remembering Cozza as a player and little league coach in Fergus Falls was the late Mark Olson, bank executive who formerly served with the Federal Reserve Board. He lived on the East Coast.

"Carmen would come down to the Athletic Park to work with me, Ron Tate and other kids," said Olson.

Tate, former businessman and educator now living in Florida, said it was great as a 10-year-old kid to get some baseball instruction from Cozza and to watch his mentor play for the local town baseball team.

"Carmen was an amazing man, and he went on to do some great things as head football coach at Yale," said Tate.

Cozza won 10 Ivy League championships in his 32 years as Yale's head football coach.

Chapter Twenty-Eight

Downtown Bowling Alley

MARY MELBY CHRISTENSON'S MEMORIES

The bowling alley in downtown Fergus Falls during the 1950s and 1960s was located near the northwest corner of Union Avenue and West Lincoln Avenue.

The entrance to the downtown bowling alley was at the left, with Our Lady of Victory Catholic Church seen in the background. Photo [# 11051] from the collections of the Otter Tail County Historical Society

Today, in 2021, the bowling alley is just a memory for long-time residents of Fergus Falls.

There were eight lanes at the old bowling alley, at the lower level. People would take stairs down to the bowling alley which also had seating for those watching the bowlers.

"That building was originally the bus depot," said Mary Melby Christenson, a 1966 graduate of Fergus Falls High School. "My grandfather had the bus service, above the bowling alley, which was Elliott Transportation."

The main level had the lunch bar, along with the ticket and waiting area. Greyhound Bus Line used to stop there.

"My grandfather later built a larger depot where Wells Fargo Bank is now located," Christenson said. "The depot was sold for the 'new' clinic on the northeast corner of South Union and East Washington, with the bank to follow at that location."

The downtown bowling alley was in the building at the time when her grandfather made the purchase. After her grandfather moved to a new location, right above the bowling alley (upstairs) was Kantruds Cafe.

"We bowled there for physical education when we were junior high students at nearby Washington School," Christenson recalls. "This building went down when the phone company expanded."

MARK ADELSMAN'S MEMORIES

Mark Adelsman, a 1967 graduate of Fergus Falls High School, remembers Satch, the bowling instructor at the downtown lanes.

"Satch was a great guy," said Adelsman. "Those were the days when kids were hired to place the pins by hand, before automatic bowling pin setter machines."

In the 1950s, when the bowler would throw the first ball, the pin setter would pick up the bowling ball and place it on the return rail. Then, as fast as he could, the pin setter would pick up the fallen pins and place them in a rack.

Then the bowler would throw a second time, unless it was a strike on the first throw.

"Those also were the days of the smoke-filled rooms," Adelsman recalled. "The bowling alley at the lower level of the building on North Union is something I look back on with fond memories."

MORE BOWLING ALLEY MEMORIES

A short distance from the downtown bowling alley was Our Lady of Victory Catholic Church. Residing in the rectory next to the church was Father Robert Smith, an avid bowler.

Father Smith and a member of his congregation, Fran Conito, bowled regularly at the downtown bowling alley. Conito was widely known in Fergus Falls as a physical education teacher at grade schools throughout the community.

The downtown bowling alley on North Union Avenue was the temporary home to the Fergus Falls YMCA, starting in 1967. Heading the YMCA in the early years was Cliff Maxwell.

The YMCA, which started with just bowling, a jukebox and a pool table at the downtown bowling alley, moved to its new home in northeast Fergus Falls in 1972.

Chapter Twenty-Nine

Edgetown

JOHN RUNNINGEN'S EDGETOWN MEMORIES

In 2021, longtime Fergus Falls residents and other Fergus Falls natives living all across the country remembered Edgetown from the 1950s and 1960s. There were buildings along the old Highway 210 near what is now the northeast section of Fleet Farm on the northwest side of Fergus Falls.

This was before the westward expansion of Fergus Falls and the construction of I-94. Included were Edgetown Lumber, International Harvester, a cabinet business, a roller skating rink and Tysdal's Livestock auction barn.

Nearby was the old radio station, with its three large towers and blinking red lights atop those towers.

"I recall Otto Korp was the owner/manager of the radio station, and quite a man about town too. Otto performed in community plays and sang solos at weddings and funerals," recalls John Runningen, a 1971 graduate of Fergus Falls High School who grew up at 1032 West Summit Avenue in Fergus Falls. He now lives in Atlanta, Georgia.

Edgetown during the 1950s at lower left included Edgetown Lumber and the Louis Tysdal Livestock auction barn. Across the road was the radio station, which is now the northeast section of Fleet Farm. Land at left center later became the campus for Fergus Falls Community College (now M State).

Photo [# 50131] from the collections of the Otter Tail County Historical Society

Runningen went to school with Korp's daughter, Linda, a talented dancer who now lives in Lynwood, California, near Los Angeles. Her brother, Scott Korp, was in Merle Atkinson's Boy Scout Troop 302 with Runningen.

"Now 50-plus years later, Scott is a friend of mine on Facebook," he said.

Other memories of Runningen's include Edgetown Lumber, managed by Ed Belka who lived on West Cavour Avenue, a stone's throw from what's now the county museum on West Lincoln Avenue.

Otto and Sue Korp, one block south at 1020 West Lincoln Avenue, were neighbors of Ed and Maguerite Belka. They were right across the street from the 25-cent laundromat and Phillips 66 station on the extreme west section of Lincoln Avenue.

"It was at Phillips 66 where we kids would get the air filled in our bike tires," Runningen recalls.

"Edgetown Lumber came to the rescue when we had to move my childhood stump house, safer and lower to the ground than a tree house," Runningen recalls. "We didn't want to tear it apart to move it."

He says the stump house was about 6 feet square, with old oak stumps holding up each corner. "We had purchased all the wood from Mr. Belka at Edgetown Lumber, so we went over to ask if he could use his forklift to move the stump house. He said 'of course,' and sent his driver over to our house," Runningen says.

"I remember it went all of 3 miles per hour, very slow indeed for an anxious boy. When he got to our house, he lifted the stump house right up, moved it about 50 feet and set it down on the new stumps that had been set up and leveled. A perfect fit."

And, emphasizes Runningen, a perfect example of how neighbors and friends helped each other out in those days. "Wouldn't that be nice in America today?"

It was at Edgetown's International Harvester where the business allowed Boy Scout Troop 302 to have a candy machine, yielding money for the troop.

Runningen, a member of the troop headed by Merle Atkinson, was responsible for filling the candy machine every week or two with licorice pieces, Virginia peanuts (the best seller), chocolate peanuts, chocolate raisins or Boston Beans.

The cost was 10 cents a box.

Troop 302 also had a candy machine at Lake Region Hospital. It was the troop's best-selling location.

"If someone sells something in a hospital, people always think it's clean and healthy. That lesson paid off very well, as I became a healthcare investment banker and analyst," Runningen says.

He also remembers the Edgetown cabinet store where owners gave kids left over pieces of wood.

"We used the wood for kindling in our fireplace," Runningen recalls. "We had a fire almost every cold night of winter. Another great childhood memory."

He recalls the roller skating rink at Edgetown that was owned by Bob Rasmusson.

"Bob's daughter, Bonnie, was in my high school class," Runningen says. "Her family members were all good roller skaters. It was much warmer than ice skating outside on Lake Alice."

He recalls the roller rink being open all year round, long after the ice on lake Alice had melted. "Great memories!"

Runningen's Closing Edgetown Thoughts

"I need to give my Grandpa Rudy Mohagen full credit for the stump house idea. He came up with that idea when he found me building a tree house in an oak tree behind our house on West Summit Avenue, 40 feet up in the air," recalls John Runningen.

Rather than reprimand John, his grandfather said, "Let me build you a really nice stump house a bit closer to the ground."

Mohagen was a good friend of Ed Belka, Edgetown Lumber manager.

"This made building the stump house easier," John said. "Grandpa Mohagen was a very wise, kind and wonderful man, and he was my best friend."

Runningen is trying to be just like his grandfather. The 1971 FFHS grad spends lots of time with his 4½-year-old grandson Reiar, son of John's daughter Nicole, who also lives in Atlanta.

"We play together every Friday when Reiar stays overnight," John says. "His Mom, my daughter, says, 'Dad, you have finally found someone your own age to play with.' She's right!"

Edgetown Facts from the County Museum

The following pages contain a summary of Edgetown provided by Vicky Anderson of the Otter Tail County Historical Society. The articles are from the *Fergus Falls Daily Journal*.

Aug. 19, 1952
Edgetown Cafe Moves to Broadway in Fergus
The cafe was moved from an alfalfa field to a site near the north end of Broadway. The project was undertaken by the Valley House Moving company of Breckenridge.

Dec. 31, 1955
Farm Equipment store to locate at Edgetown
International Harvester Company has announced the purchase of a tract of land at Edgetown. The company bought a tract 250 feet wide and 372 feet deep which includes the Sandness building next to the Auction Market.

The establishment, to be known as the McCormick Farm Equipment store, will open sometime in February. It will provide parts service and new goods in farm equipment and motor trucks.

June 22, 1959
Roller rink to be built
Construction started today on a roller skating rink at the west edge of Edgetown. Bob Rasmusson, the owner, said completion is expected by July 31. The contractors, Lunde and Wallin, began work on the foundation after ground was leveled.

The building will be 60 by 120 in size. The floor will be concrete with a plastic coating. The building will be of frame construction.

Sept. 16, 1959
Grand Opening

It's another Rolling Roller Rink! Edgetown Area West Fergus Falls across from the Radio Station West on Highway 210. Friday, Sept. 18. Skating every Sunday, Tuesday and Friday nights from 8 to 11 p.m. And Sunday afternoons from 2 to 4:30 p.m.

Aug. 23, 1963
Business grows on 210 West

Fergus Falls isn't involved in the suburban sprawl of a metropolis but there's been lots of growth outside the city limits. Primarily the growth has been along highways.

A few more tracts of farmland along Highway 210 West of Fergus Falls will disappear and both sides of the highway all the way to the Interstate 94 will be taken over by businesses.

Edgetown, the name given to the area about 15 years ago, started with Lewis Tysdal's Auction Market and Edgetown Lumber.

Oct. 28, 1964
Jr. College site approved

After months of consideration the school board approved acquisition of 148 acres northwest of the McKinley elementary school. The area presently is farmland. It is near the end of several city streets and adjoins Highway 210 near Edgetown.

Oct. 27, 1966
Lampert buys Fergus Lumber and Fuel Co.

The family-owned Fergus Lumber was started by the late C. G. Rosengren, 60 years ago, until the sale to Lampert.

Lampert Lumber Company, headquartered in St. Paul, owns Edgetown Lumber and 60 to 65 lumberyards in Minnesota, Nebraska, North and South Dakota.

Lampert Lumber Company announced the purchase of the Fergus Lumber and Fuel Company at 324 East Washington. Lampert will close its Stanton Avenue yard in its move to provide better service and more facilities.

It has operated a lumberyard in Fergus Falls for 30 years. Manager Howard Knight will continue as manager of the new yard. Don Husfeldt is the assistant manager.

July 23, 1969
Edgetown lumber sets open house

Edgetown Lumber Company has been in business on old Highway 210 at the west edge of Fergus Falls since 1948 but the establishment looks brand new for its open house. A new front has been added.

The sales room is new with a number of lines never offered before at Edgetown, including kitchen and bathroom fixtures, paint, hardware, lighting fixtures, carpeting and other types of floor covering.

Manager Ed Belka said the aim is to provide one-stop service for customers

Jul 11, 1994
Duo put experience to work
There's a new kid on the block–or rather, a new used car lot at Edgetown. But the owners aren't new to the business at all. Larry Peasley, sales, and Phillip Kugler, mechanic, are the co-owners and have 27 years of experience between them, both having worked for Worners Auto Sales Inc. in Fergus Falls.

Opening College Way Auto is a dream come true for them. On the site of what used to be Edgetown Lumber Company, the 60-by-1000 foot metal building that was used for storing insulation has now been completely remodeled by Peasley and Kugler.

Feb 10, 2015
City of Fergus Falls demolishes former Edgetown Arena roller rink building

Chapter Thirty

Sharp Farm near Everdell

by Sherry Mjelde Landrud

PULLING UP ROOTS

Bessie and Earl Sharp, along with their children Chester, Harry and Gene, pulled up their roots and moved from their prairie farm near Aberdeen, South Dakota, to a farm they rented near Breckenridge in the early 1930s.

My Grandma Bessie shared with me as a young child the day this decision became reality.

She was eager to "deep clean" her South Dakota farm home because four of her favorite cousins were driving from Saskatchewan, Canada, to visit her family, their first visit together in several years.

Grandma Bessie had just finished cleaning the main floor, including hanging all of the heavy rugs out on the clothesline, pounding out the dust, lugging them back inside, and then washing, ironing and re-hanging all of the curtains.

While admiring her clean first floor, she opened the windows in each room slightly to let in the fresh air breeze and then ascended upstairs to tackle cleaning the second floor.

As she started cleaning their bedroom, Grandma Bessie heard the eerie dust bowl winds starting to blow, swirling up mini-dust funnels that filled the air with thick sandy dust clouds. Glancing out the window, she knew she had to quickly run downstairs to close the windows.

Standing on the bottom stair step she already knew that she was too late.

Grandma Bessie, a small 88-pound woman, short and petite in stature but strong in spirit, glanced around the main floor. Dusty sand covered every conceivable living space.

She dropped down on the gritty floor and sobbed as her husband, Earl, walked in from the stormy fields. She announced to her husband, "This Dust Bowl is ruining our family and we can no longer survive here."

That very day they made plans to leave their South Dakota homestead. Unfortunately, their four Canadian cousins were unable to ever visit them there due to the dire conditions from the Dust Bowl.

PUTTING DOWN NEW ROOTS

The Sharp family purged their belongings as much as possible for the journey in the early 1930s to unseen territory in northwest Minnesota, where they hoped to put down roots for a second time.

Among their belongings they brought along were a heavy family upright player piano and a lovely oak library table, my grandma's favorite piece of furniture. The piano is in the home of their fourth-generation great-granddaughter, Greta, and their granddaughter, Sherry, now has the coveted library table, still stacked high with treasured books.

The Sharp farm in the early days near Everdell,
between Foxhome and Breckenridge

They rented a 400-acre farm in Wilkin County, just east of Breckenridge near the town of Everdell, with rich, black soil – some of the best in the land. The farmstead included a five-bedroom, boxy white farmhouse with wooden steps leading up the open porch.

Three barns, a granary, chicken coop, garage, pump house, artesian well in the front yard and a row of storage bins and corn cribs were all visible alongside the gravel road coming into the farm.

Uncle Harry later also built an octagon machinery shed by the other barns to house and protect the machinery, especially during the harsh winters. People often drove by to see his unique design, the first in the area.

The Sharps added Guernsey milking cows (Grandpa Sharp chose this variety because they were known for the high level of fat in their rich milk), a few pigs, sheep and baby lambs to their family, as well as two dogs and several farm cats.

Grandma Sharp and her daughter, my mother Gene, also raised chickens and sold the eggs each Saturday in Breckenridge. With the egg proceeds they purchased a 12-piece set of formal dining dishes, "Stansbury Federal" Syracuse china, a few pieces each week. After 18 months they had a full set of fancy dishes for dining, their first real luxury, including two sizes of serving platters and a gravy boat. To this day, these dishes are used on holidays and special occasions and are fondly known as "the egg dishes."

The gravel road coming into the farm passed a collection of white wooden boxes, stacked up in precise fashion, the bee keepers plot, with his guarantee of as much honey as Grandma Sharp could use each year for cooking and baking. Little did Burt the beekeeper know that Grandma Sharp would use gallons of honey as a sugar substitute for everything!

Initially, when the Sharps started farming east of Breckenridge near Everdell, they used horses to plow the fields and continued these practices into the late 1940s and early 1950s.

Uncle Harry was partial to Minneapolis Moline tractors and they bought two of these tractors, one for Grandpa Sharp and another for Uncle Harry as they transitioned to machinery. They initially used threshing machines to harvest grain and later transitioned to John Deere 105 combines.

When they started out farming the fields, they grew crops of oats, barley, corn and wheat. Later they added crops of soybeans and sunflowers. Now mostly soybeans, wheat, corn and sugar beets are grown. Sugar beets came into the area in the early 1970s when the Minn-Dak Farmers Cooperative was formed. Uncle Harry was one of the last farmers in the area to grow flax and sweet clover.

With successful crops and frugal fiscal management, Earl and Bessie were able to eventually purchase 840 acres. As their health declined in their later years, Uncle Harry assumed responsibility for farming the entire 840 acres with minimal assistance, except during harvest time.

Bessie Sharp, about 1935, leaving the chicken coop while holding onto a chicken

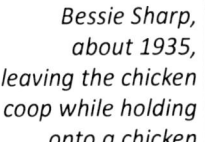

Sherry Mjelde in 1955 with Grandma Bessie Sharp and Grandpa Earl Sharp

Gene Sharp on her tricycle at the Everdell farm, about 1932

He was known for his mechanical and engineering skills, and was generally considered as someone who was always willing to adopt new farming technology and methods.

When my grandparents and Harry passed away, the farm was rented out to the Hasbargen and Beyer families. My grandparents and Uncle Harry enjoyed a good relationship with their farm neighbors, notably the Beyer family.

Today 400 acres, including the homestead, are still owned by the Sharp's grandchildren, Myron Mjelde and Sherry (Mjelde) Landrud. The balance of the farm was sold to the Hasbargen and Beyer families.

The Sharp Farm Memories that Gave Me Roots

My initial memories of my grandparent's farm were the weekly Sunday visits there after my parents closed The Neighborhood Grocery in Fergus Falls at noon.

My mom packed groceries into several sturdy bags to bring to my grandparents and Uncle Harry. Mom saved fruit and vegetables, now slightly too ripe or blemished to sell, to bring to my grandmother's kitchen. Grandma Sharp would know exactly what to do with a dozen overly ripe bananas or blemished Jonathan apples!

In addition to these filled bags, there was the typical fare for their week ahead, packed with the organized rhythm of Mom and Dad's bustling style in anticipation of the delicious Sunday dinner down on the farm, served promptly at 1 p.m.

We looked forward to this cherished Sunday ritual all week as we locked the main door to the store and quickly scampered into our car, packed to overflowing, smelling like ripe bananas!

The drive out to the Sharp farm near the Otter Tail River (which later flows into the Red River) was about 25 minutes from Fergus Falls. Passing familiar landmarks every Sunday like precision clockwork assured me that we were on the right course and would be on time for the big meal.

With our collective stomachs growling, we all rejoiced as we passed the Everdell sign and, shortly thereafter, turned south onto the bumpy gravel road, which meant we were close. We viewed the weekly progress of the growing crops, soybeans on one side and corn on the other, almost ready for harvesting.

I could see the farmstead ahead on the southwest side of the gravel road, a boxy farmhouse with a front porch, a white glimmer against the noon sun.

When we stepped up the gray concrete steps into the roomy mudroom, we noted an array of hooks for seasonal farm clothing and boot trays ready to house muddy footwear. The huge white enamel sink had a longneck grey spigot with stacked bars of Lava soap for scrubbing my Grandpa and Uncle Harry's dirt-grimed skin from a long day in the dusty farm fields.

On the opposite wall were two large freezers, one an upright, filled to the brim with Grandma's berries, vegetables, baked bread, cookies and various kinds of homemade pies. The other, a large chest freezer, housed beef, chickens, pheasants and ducks, labeled and wrapped in white butcher paper, all once former habitants of the premises.

The smells whiffling from around the corner of Grandma Sharp's kitchen as you entered the mudroom confirmed every single Sunday at 1 p.m. that this was truly going to be THE best meal of our week!

Slamming the side door as I walked up the side stoop (as my Grandma Sharp called the cement steps), I glanced at the ladder-back antique chairs, sniffed the smells coming from the kitchen, and knew exactly what our 1 p.m. Sunday dinner would be, one of my favorites!

Drying on the backs of several antique ladder-back chairs in the mudroom were long, (about 3 feet), thin strips of pastry, and I knew instantly dinner today would be her homemade egg noodles with a few of her stewed chickens in homemade chicken broth.

She greeted us with hugs as my parents and Uncle Harry looked for spaces to put the grocery bags in an already crowded kitchen, with counters cluttered from the Sunday dinner preparations.

The dining room table, visible from the open kitchen, was already set for us with a small crock of three varieties of her lovely iris flowers, my Grandma's favorite variety.

She would take me every Sunday when they were in bloom to her half-acre vegetable and flower garden behind the farmhouse. Grandma had a clear view of the irises from her kitchen window, where all 88 pounds of her wiry little body stood tirelessly, prepping meals and washing dishes for thrashers every fall. She often told me she never tired of the iris' hues in view.

The dining room table, waiting for company, was adorned with Grandma's homemade signature food items from her stocked cellar: halved gingered peaches, dill and sweet pickles, beet pickles, apple butter, and strawberry/rhubarb and orange marmalade jellies. Sliced radishes in a pretty flowered dish, with salt and butter on the side, were waiting next to my Grandpa Earl's head position at the table, his favorite!

My brother, Myron, scampered into the living room, eager to play with Uncle Harry's cast iron toy tractors, while I washed my hands, pleased to be asked to help Grandma gather the pastry strips into the one cleared-off bare spot on the kitchen counter.

I watched her methodically snip the large egg noodle strips into pieces, dip them in batches into two pots of stewing chickens and watched the broth quickly thicken and bubble up. She added more than a generous "pinch" of salt and pepper and a fresh clump of tied parsley from her garden for added flavor as we were all called to the table.

My favorite Sunday meal consisted of delicious chicken in a rich broth with the thick homemade egg noodles, homemade warm bread for dipping or slathering with jams, fresh green dilled beans from her garden, and gooseberry Jell-O, (a recipe she'd concocted with lime Jell-O as she wondered what could be done with the ripe gooseberry bunches growing by her back door).

After our bellies were full from the main course, my Grandma Sharp brought out her three-layer fresh strawberry pies with generous globs of homemade whipped cream. Even though my Grandma "ate like a bird" with the tiniest dinner portions on her plate imaginable, she loved sweets and always cut one-quarter of a pie piece for herself.

Grandma told my mom and me she was "deliciously tired" as we helped with all of the dishes from the meal and the morning's kitchen clutter. I loved listening to the conversations between Grandma Sharp and my mom as they caught up on the news of the week.

While we were doing the dishes, their party line phone rang, one short and two longs to the ring. This party line was shared among five farm families nearby. My grandma picked it up, even though it was not their "number" of three shorts and one long. My grandma asked my mom and I to listen to the conversation and to be very still while doing so.

My grandparents and my Uncle Harry were all hard of hearing and wore clunky pocket-pack hearing aids that buzzed when they were set on the table. They could never hear their farm neighbor's phone conversations (it was a known fact that on their party line EVERYONE listened to one another's "private" conversations) on a static party line with compromised acoustic quality.

This was my initial immersion into the world of those hard of hearing, impacted by their self-identified social isolation, yearning to know the gossip and news of the farmers nearby but often left out of the "goings on of one another," as Grandma Sharp would often say.

Sharp Farm Memories
Rooted Through the Generations

Over the years, we continued to make weekly Sunday visits to the farm and ate the best meal we had all week, cooked by Grandma Sharp with their chickens and beef, garden produce, homemade breads and desserts and canned goods from her pantry.

I remember favorite foods, and now wish I would have jotted down the recipes for these treasured dishes. Also, I wish that I would have watched Grandma Sharp can and had written down those recipes.

I remember rides in the farm fields with my brother and Dad as Grandpa Sharp, in his Studebaker car, drove us around to check on the crops each week. The faces of the lush sunflowers seemed to follow us around the fields, changing their position as the sun went down.

In the summer months, we checked to see if the corn was truly "knee high by the 4th of July." We would often get out of the car, stand in the field near the corn and measure the height!

The Otter Tail River, bordering the farm for about one-half mile as it flowed westward toward the Red River of the North, was always interesting to observe as the seasons changed. In the fall, Grandma Sharp gave us first choice to pick our Halloween pumpkins from her bountiful half-acre vegetable and flower garden.

I remember pheasant and duck hunting season when men (including my cousin Tom Hintgen) and boys came to hunt on the farm, and I was able to assist Grandma Sharp in preparing their evening meal after hunting. She often made her signature dinner for the hunters – roast pheasant in cream sauce – and it was a favorite of all who gathered. She always had at least two kinds of homemade pies, served in hearty portions with her homemade ice cream for their dessert.

I remember remedies that Grandma Sharp knew and demonstrated, such as washing down fruit trees with Fels Naptha soap to keep the bugs away from the fruit. When my Dad had a chest cold, Grandma Sharp would make a paste of ginger root and fresh mustard from her garden and spread it on his chest. He claimed that it was very warm with a deep aroma that seemed to suppress his coughing.

Each Sunday we watched all of the TV show, *Lassie*, and the beginning of the *Ed Sullivan Show* before it was time to pack up and head back to Fergus Falls. Myron and I would typically fall asleep in the car on the ride home and Dad would carry us to our beds, our bellies full of great food and our hearts full of fond memories.

Even to this day when I garden, I think of Grandma Sharp and the image of her tiny, petite frame with her large bare hands, buried in her garden, muddy and black, the rich dirt in every crevasse and under every fingernail.

She always told me that real gardeners must touch the earth with their bare hands, for this was the only way that gardening "would root you, and touch your soul."

She was little bitty, 88 pounds and cared for a half-acre garden full of produce and irises, canned it all, cooked for threshers and cared for a five-bedroom house. She only sat on Sunday after the meal. So on those days when I touch the earth in my garden, I think of her; I feel rooted and I know she has touched my soul, rooted through the generations.

In this painting, Gene Sharp, daughter of Bessie and Earl Sharp, wears an outfit her Mom made for her, including the bonnet and leggings. She is bottle feeding her pet lamb, Wheatie (named because the lamb was the color of the wheat growing in the fields). Gene loved this pet lamb because she was very lonely, living on the farm with two brothers considerably older than she was.

Painting by Scott Gunvaldson, Fergus Falls, MN
(See original color painting on front cover)

Chapter Thirty-One

Colbecks, Hillcrest

SCOTT COLBECK'S MEMORIES

Scott Colbeck has fond memories of growing up in the old Hillcrest Academy gymnasium. His father, Bill Colbeck, was his high school coach.

"My best memories aren't so much of playing in the actual games, but more so of the endless hours attending my dad's practices as a little boy," he said, "sitting on the bench as the water boy, or the hours spent in the gym by myself."

During the summer when the school was locked, Bill Colbeck would give his son Scott the keys to the building.

"I had unlimited access to the gym," Scott says, "and it was my favorite place."

He says his childhood memories include coming home from Adams School and heading straight to the gym to watch practice.

"I was allowed to dribble and shoot on the side baskets as long as the ball didn't end up on the court."

Hillcrest Lutheran Academy, the castle on the hill

"Assistant Coach Richard Risbrudt gave me my first varsity start (second half) five games into my sophomore season when the head coach (my dad, Bill Colbeck) was home with the flu."

Both Bill Colbeck and Scott Colbeck are members of the Fergus Falls Chamber of Commerce Sports Hall of Fame.

"To this day, my favorite place to be is still in a gymnasium," said Scott, elementary principal for the Fergus Falls Public School system in 2020."

"Whether watching my own children play or officiating high school basketball games, there's a certain comfort level I have with being in that setting."

Scott, in addition to playing basketball for his father at Hillcrest, played basketball for Fergus Falls Community College (now M State) and the University of Minnesota, Morris. He was captain for the Fergus Falls-based Spartans, coached by Dave Retzlaff, another member of the Chamber Hall of Fame.

Colbeck had many basketball honors while playing for all three of the aforementioned teams.

He holds a Master's Degree in Educational Leadership from Minnesota State University, Moorhead, and is a Fergus Falls principal for McKinley and Adams schools.

Colbeck and his wife, Debbie, have three children: Caitlyn, Elijah and Ellie.

REMEMBERING BILL COLBECK

Bill Colbeck, the father of Scott Colbeck, was a native of Chicago.

He turned down a scholarship offer to play basketball at the University of Michigan. Instead, he attended one year of pre-seminary at Lutheran Brethren Seminary in Fergus Falls.

Colbeck graduated from Brooklyn College and in 1959 returned to Fergus Falls to complete his seminary training by 1962.

He coached Hillcrest Comet basketball, and in 1974 his team won the National Christian Invitational Tournament in Arkansas.

Hillcrest, as a private school, joined the Minnesota State High School League in 1976. That same year the Comets won the District 23 basketball title in Moorhead.

Colbeck took on duties as Hillcrest principal in 1964. He also coached baseball and track at the academy, in addition to basketball.

The three children of the late Bill and Joy Colbeck are Susan, Dawn and Scott. Scott and sisters Dawn and Susan played basketball for the Comets.

AUTHOR'S RECOLLECTIONS

My late father, Roy Hintgen, employed many Hillcrest Academy students to deliver stoves and refrigerators for Hintgen-Karst Electric in downtown Fergus Falls.

The Hillcrest students had the first offers for these after-school jobs, since classes at Hillcrest ended earlier in the day compared to the public schools.

My father was close to the administrators at Hillcrest and to Church of the Lutheran Brethren as a whole. As a Catholic he made it a point to learn more about other denominations, saying, "We all worship the same God."

It was a thrill for me to cover Comet basketball games as a stringer for the *Fergus Falls Daily Journal* while attending school in the late 1960s, and as a full-time *Daily Journal* employee from 1972 to 1977.

I felt fortunate to cover the Comet basketball games in 1974, the year Hillcrest won the national title in Arkansas.

Through the year 2000 I attended Hillcrest Comet basketball games in the old gym, and I'm glad they have preserved this classic, small arena.

I like to compare the old Hillcrest gym to the Hoosier gym in Knightstown, Indiana, where the classic movie was filmed in 1986.

The arena in Indiana, used from 1921 to 1966, is preserved and attracts close to 80,000 visitors a year.

I remember when the first class from the Danielson School in Norway came to study at Hillcrest in Fergus Falls in 1989.

Each spring, at graduation, the students from Norway received certificates following their junior year of study. Those awards were given during the Hillcrest high school graduation ceremony. The students then returned to Norway for their senior year of high school.

Danielsen Schools are Christian private schools, mainly based in Bergen, Norway. My wife, Sharon, and I visited Bergen in 2017, during a tour of Scandinavia. It was nice to see where the Danielson School is located.

Chapter Thirty-Two

Camp Nidaros

CAMP NIDAROS NEAR WALKER LAKE

Camp Nidaros near Walker Lake, north of Otter Tail Lake, is in a sense an old neighborhood at one of Otter Tail County's more than 1,000 lakes.

This lake neighborhood has its roots in the purchase of property back in 1909 by the original founders of Camp Nidaros. They were mainly involved with the ministry, built cabins and formed an association.

The camp is located six miles west of Ottertail city on a peninsula between Otter Tail Lake and Walker Lake.

Of the 16 cottages, 14 are owned by family members of the original owners.

Stan Satre has been the main chaplain at Camp Nidaros since 1992, heading many of the 10 a.m. Sunday worship services himself and also lining up other speakers. He rings the bell at 9:30 a.m. and again at 9:55 a.m. as a final reminder for worshipers prior to the start of the service.

In 2021 Stan, 89, was the pastor for all four outdoor Sunday worship services during the month of July. Most of

Each summer Pastor Stan Satre calls nearby lake cabin dwellers to the outdoor Sunday morning worship by ringing this bell at Camp Nidaros near Walker Lake.

the pastors who used to fill in for Stan have passed away or are in unstable health.

His wife Bev's great-grandfather, Martin Soelberg, was the builder of the first four cabins more than a century ago. Her parents, with help from Stan and Bev's brother, built their current cabin back in 1956.

Stan and Bev met during their collegiate years at St. Olaf College in Northfield and were married in 1954. Stan, ordained as a minister at Luther Seminary in St. Paul in 1958, served in the ministry at several locations across the United States.

He retired with Bev in Fergus Falls in 2006, serving local churches on an interim basis.

"The summer of 2019 was noteworthy with the purchase of new outdoor cedar benches for our place of worship," Satre said.

Over the years, in addition to regular Sunday morning worship services, the site has also been used for weddings and baptisms. If it rains, people come to the Satre cabin, which can accommodate from 40 to 50 worshipers.

"Our open-air services at Camp Nidaros have been very special over the years," Stan said. "The tradition of outdoor services is passed from generation to generation."

From 40 to 50 people attend outdoor worship at Camp Nidaros on any given Sunday during the summer months.

During the colder months, Stan and Bev reside at West Alcott Avenue in Fergus Falls and also head south for a while during the winter months.

They have five daughters, four of whom met their husbands at St. Olaf College. Stan and Bev have 18 grand-children.

"We're blessed to have our kids and grandchildren stay with us often here at the lake," Satre said.

Bev recalls the old days at Camp Nidaros during the 1940s, when kerosene lamps were used in the cabin. Two of those lamps are displayed today at their cabin.

She says that the word "camp" is really a misnomer since, in reality, Camp Nidaros has always been a spot away from home for pastors and their families, many of them educators.

Chapter Thirty-Three

OLV School

OLV SCHOOL OPENED IN THE FALL OF 1956

In 2020, Gary Jennen, Michelle Simons Lindquist and Richard Tomhave paused after Mass in front of Our Lady of Victory School (OLV) and recalled the fall of 1956 when the school opened its doors for the first time.

These three parishioners became OLV students as 4th graders for the 1956-57 school year.

Jennen and Tomhave were raised on farms west of Fergus Falls. Michelle Simons Lindquist grew up on East Summit Avenue. After her marriage to John Lindquist, she became a farm wife near Dalton where she and John operated a dairy farm.

OLV School is located near the northwest corner of Vine Street and Cavour Avenue, just northwest of downtown Fergus Falls.

"This school has certainly withstood the test of time," Jennen said. "The school was built very well back in the 1950s, and that's reflective of what we have today."

These former OLV School classmates, (l-r) Gary Jennen, Michelle Simons Lindquist and Richard Tomhave, recalled their first year at the school as fourth graders in 1956-57.
Gary and Richard grew up on farms. Michelle was raised in the city and later, through marriage, became a farm wife.

During the first three years of operation, OLV School conducted classes for grades one through six. The school also had classes for 7th and 8th graders from 1960 to 1968.

During the 1960s, all classes (with the exception of 7th grade, taught by Karleen Wollmering), were taught by the Franciscan Sisters, whose campus and retirement home is in Little Falls.

The convent that housed the sisters was in the northwest section of the block, where the church is now located. The old church was in the opposite section of the block, where the school playground is now situated.

Sister Adela Gross, formerly known as Sister Mary Peter, was the 8th-grade teacher and principal for Jennen, Lindquist and Tomhave in 1960-61. In 2021, she resided at the retirement home in Little Falls.

Back in the late 1950s and early 1960s, students were required to have number 2 pencils and were supplied with penmanship pens. They sat at plastic-composite desks with chrome legs.

Those were the days of the Cold War between the United States and the Soviet Union. OLV students had classroom breaks when they were served half pints of milk.

Lindquist remembers recess when, on nice winter days, OLV students would shoot marbles. "We had our own little marble tournaments," she says.

Jennen recalls the same playground where students played dodgeball, had hula hoops, and more than one student had a Yo-Yo, a toy consisting of an axle connected to two disks and a string looped around the axle.

"We played king of the hill during the winter where we had snow piles near the school," Jennen recalled. "Early on the playground was gravel covered, so in the spring we could make river dams in the gravel."

Tomhave later became an active member of the Knights of Columbus (KC), who held bingo games in the OLV gymnasium. The KCs also held pancake breakfasts in the gym adjacent to the school, which he attended from 1956-57 (4th grade) to 1960-61 (8th grade).

Houses were on the north side of the school, to the east of the convent. The parish rectory was north of the old church, on Vine Street. There was another house north of the rectory.

Many OLV School alums also recall fun times in the 1950s and 1960s over the noon hour at the nearby Athletic Park where soccer was popular. A few kids at the park even snuck in cap guns, which were toy guns that created loud sounds and a puff of smoke.

Gary, Michelle and Richard, whose children also attended classes at Our Lady of Victory School, give rave reviews to lunchroom director Esther Spranger. She cooked turkey dinners, with all the trimmings, prior to the Thanksgiving break.

Their class also had a great basketball player, the late Tony Silbernagel. In those days, in the early 1960s, there was a traveling 7th- and 8th-grade basketball team, coached by John Schrom. There also were OLV cheerleaders.

OLV played other area Catholic schools on Sunday afternoons, including parochial schools in Breckenridge, Barnesville, Perham, Morris and Wadena. The late Mike Wilkinson, OLV class of 1962, also was a star basketball player.

Many former OLV students, such as Linda Earle Lorenz, a member of the OLV class of 1962, recall the 8th-grade class trips to Duluth, shortly before graduation. "I still have photos of that trip to Duluth, and have good memories of my education at Our Lady of Victory School," says Lorentz, a current resident of Alexandria.

Former OLV altar boys recall 4th-grade teacher, Sister Mary Christine, teaching Latin to them over the noon hours. Those were the days of the Latin Masses.

This changed in 1962, following the Second Vatican Council, with the Mass changing worldwide from Latin to vernacular languages. The Mass thus changed to English in the United States.

OLV School also had a school safety patrol on duty when students entered crosswalks before and after school.

Many students also were members of Boy Scout Troop 312, sponsored by the Knights of Columbus. Scoutmaster in the late 1950s and early 1960s was Tom Donoho.

Former scouts remember fundraising pancake and sausage feeds held at the OLV cafeteria on some weekday evenings. They were highly successful, raising money for scout trips to Camp Wilderness near Park Rapids in both the summer and winter.

Kathy Scheidecker Warn, who lived just west of OLV School, also has fond memories. She was in the 8th-grade class of 1962. "I can hardly believe it's been so many years since we were students at OLV," she said in 2020. "Recently I was going through stuff from my childhood here in the Twin Cities and found spelling, handwriting, geography, math, etc., workbooks from grades 6, 7 and 8. I looked through them with good memories."

SCHEIDECKER FAMILY MEMORIES OF NEARBY ATHLETIC PARK

Two beautiful benches are located at the softball and baseball field at T.H. Johnson (Athletic) Park on North Vine Street in Fergus Falls, just north of Our Lady of Victory School in Fergus Falls. On each bench are the words, "In Loving memory of Roy Scheidecker, 1923-2003."

Roy, who worked at Otter Tail Power Company in the accounting department before his retirement, was 79 when he died on January 1, 2003. The benches were installed by his family the following year.

During World War II, Roy served with the U.S. Navy. He was a radio operator, spending time on the *USS Missouri*. His service included action in Guam and the South Pacific.

"I remember many hours of fun with Dad at the Athletic Park, close to our house on West Cavour near Our Lady of Victory (OLV) School, playing catch with a ball and glove or throwing footballs," said his youngest son, Craig. "He simply liked being around sporting events."

A daughter, Connie Scheidecker Torgerson, said that her father, a few years before his death, was watching his grandsons (Brett, Drew and Grant) play baseball at the Athletic Park. Roy pointed out where benches, at some time, should be placed.

"Dad wanted the benches just behind home plate, at an angle so you could see and hear the (umpire) calls," she said.

"As kids we called the Athletic Park 'Cathletic' Park, since we also spent time at the park as part of OLV School recess and lunchtime activities."

Roy was a native of Perham. In high school he played football as an offensive lineman. The benches, positioned at the Athletic Park in his memory, reflect his love for athletics.

His oldest child, Kathy Scheidecker Warn (OLV 8th-grade class of 1962), said Roy watched many hours of her brothers' ballgames at the Athletic Park. Later, he watched his grandchildren play ball at the park and participate at the nearby tennis courts.

Roy watched grandson Rob, son of Kathy and husband Bob Warn, play tennis at the Athletic Park.

"I spent many hours at the Athletic Park green house that stored games and supplies during the summer months. We learned to braid with plastic laces used for keys or lanyard for a whistle," Warn said.

"In fact, I used the last one I made during my years as a teacher to call kids in from the playground. My brothers played carroms endlessly in the afternoon at the greenhouse during the summer."

Chapter Thirty-Four

Les, Lloyd and Rodney Anderson

TWIN BROTHERS CAME TO FERGUS IN 1965

The fall of 1965 was an exciting time for twin brothers Les and Lloyd Anderson, who became Fergus Falls residents with their family at 401 West Vasa Avenue.

They came to town as high school juniors after their father, A. LeRoy Anderson, transferred from Elbow Lake to Fergus Falls as an employee of Otter Tail Power Company.

Also living at the southwest corner of West Vasa and South Vine Street were their mother, Helen, and younger brother Rodney. Three blocks to the west was Hillcrest Academy and three blocks to the east was Lake Region Hospital.

The twins quickly acclimated to Fergus Falls High School, found new friends, did well in the classroom and participated in athletics.

Les eventually became a starter for the Otter boys basketball team, of which Lloyd also was a member. In the spring Lloyd excelled with Otter baseball.

Twins Les and Lloyd Anderson and their younger brother, Rodney, resided at 401 West Vasa in Fergus Falls.

They played basketball for two head coaches at FFHS – Ken Naffziger in 1965-66 and Dennis Anderson in 1966-67.

In their senior year, Les was named all-conference and the Otter Bruce Award winner in basketball. Lloyd was named the Otter baseball team MVP.

Les and Lloyd then attended Fergus Falls Junior College (now M State). They graduated from the junior college and then obtained engineering degrees at the University of Minnesota, graduating in 1971.

Les attained a mechanical engineering degree and Lloyd graduated with a degree in electrical engineering.

"We were at the age when young men faced the draft for Vietnam (the first draft that was done live on TV). Our draft number (birthdate) was drawn as number 29, so we were pretty much assured of being drafted," Les said.

"We were granted deferments until graduation, as long as we maintained progress towards our degrees in the standard time."

They applied for and were accepted into the Navy Officer Candidate Program.

Les joined the Navy in January 1972 and he was commissioned as an officer in May 1972. His base station was in Hawaii.

"Later that year the ship I was stationed on was deployed to Vietnam," he said.

Lloyd was commissioned as an officer in late 1972 and was stationed as a systems analyst in Pearl Harbor, Hawaii.

Les went to sea on a destroyer in and around the Vietnam theatre. After his sea duty, he and Lloyd were stationed together at Camp Smith in Hawaii for the final year of their military commitment.

While at the University of Minnesota, Les interned at NSP (now Xcel Energy) and started full-time after graduation until he left for the Navy.

"When my Navy commitment ended, I landed a job as a mechanical engineer at the Prairie Island nuclear plant near Red Wing," Les said.

He held both a registered professional engineer license and NRC senior reactor operator license. Retirement came in 2005, although he returned to work at the plant as a contractor on and off for a few years.

Les and Glenda, both from Fergus Falls, as of 2021 still resided in Red Wing. They have three children and three grandchildren.

"I spend most of the summer sailing on Lake Pepin and in the winter I enjoy woodcarving," he said. "Glenda enjoys her knitting and gardening."

Twin brother Lloyd, after completing his Naval service, took a job offer in Washington, D.C.

"Over the next 30 years I worked on major systems programs in the DC area as a contractor, and almost 25 years as a government manager," he said.

Lloyd retired from the Department of Homeland Security in 2009, and then worked at a think tank in McLean, Virginia, until 2014.

In 2021 he and his wife, Lynn, resided near Montross, Virginia. They have two sons and two grandchildren.

Lloyd enjoys golfing and fishing. Lynn enjoys spinning and weaving various types of crafts.

As for Rod, he graduated from FFHS in 1973. From there he attended the University of Minnesota and obtained a degree in electrical engineering with high distinction.

After graduation, he was hired by Texas Instruments, Inc., in Houston, Texas, and worked as an electrical engineer. In the evenings, he attended University of Houston Law School and subsequently graduated Magna Cum Laude.

He's practiced as a patent attorney for many years, including at his own firm in Dallas, Texas. Rod and his wife, Dalia, have two children and three grandchildren.

Chapter Thirty-Five

Gary & Karalyn Harrington Farm Memories

THE HARRINGTONS

This chapter includes a husband and wife who both grew up on farms and who met while attending Fergus Falls Junior College, which later was known as the community college and is now part of M State. Karalyn went on to graduate from Moorhead State University. Gary, after completing military service, graduated from the University of Minnesota with an engineering degree.

Gary Harrington was raised on a farm near Phelps Mill, and Karalyn grew up on a farm north of Fergus Falls.

They spent their working years in the Twin Cities employed by international corporations, Karalyn in the field of Human Resources and Gary in Marketing and Marketing Communications. They raised two sons and retired to give back through involvement in endeavors such as economic development and other civic involvement.

They were happy to expand on the words written in the prologue to this book, which included the following:

Those who grew up on area farms refer to working alongside family members while doing farm chores, working with animals from chickens to horses, taking the opportunities to watch sunrises and sunsets, loving country school, 4-H and friends on nearby farms.

Gary Harrington recalls his memories in the next section of this chapter, followed by memories of his wife, Karalyn.

Gary Harrington with his 4-H hogs. He won Jr. Grand Championship with his Duroc hog and raised the second hog for his family to butcher.

HANSON-HARRINGTON FARM, MAINE TOWNSHIP

Gary Harrington grew up on his grandparents' small 160-acre dairy farm where his grandparents (on his mother's side) and his family of six had houses not 50 yards apart.

The farm property, located in Maine Township just northeast of Phelps Mill, was purchased by his grandfather, Henry W. Hanson, in 1936.

"My grandparents farmed the land and my father and mother, Bruce and Romayne, had a trucking business, based from the farm property," Gary said. "Their business was mainly focused on hauling livestock each week to the South St. Paul Stockyards."

Some of Gary's greatest memories living on the farm include raising 4-H hogs, trapping gophers and carrying his Daisy® BB gun all over the farm.

"When I think back to farm life, one special touch and smell that comes back vividly is being around the soft and loveable Holstein calves," he said. "Bringing some of those calves into the world wasn't always easy."

He recalls helping his grandfather when birthing became difficult for a cow. "We would tie a rope on whatever part of the calf that was protruding and brace ourselves on something on the barn floor, pulling with all our power to bring the calf into the world before it suffocated."

Each summer two of his mother's sisters and their families from the Chicago suburbs visited the farm for an entire week.

"It was great to have them around, but it was too short a time frame to truly introduce those city-dwelling cousins into all aspects of farm life. Boy, did we try, however."

*Gary's mother and her sisters loved to prepare a basket lunch
and take the kids out to the cattle pasture for a picnic.
Looking back, Gary is sure those picnics also are childhood memories
for his sisters who also grew up on the farm.*

*The two Harrington sisters, Gail and Jean (on left), and Gary
show one of their Chicago cousins how to make Minnesota mud pies.*

The farmyard in 1954
Note Gary's grandmother standing in the barn door, at right.
The silo seemed so large while growing up but, in reality, it was
extremely small. The barn was large enough for storing enough
winter silage for the herd of only 14 dairy cows.

Farm yard photo of
Grandfather Henry
Hanson with Gary's
siblings, Jean, Kevin
and Gail.

Gary has special baseball memories, starting early in life.

"In our rural country school, I recall only one other boy who had a baseball glove and he would play catch with me. There were no neighbor kids close to the farm who would have been around to play catch with on weekends."

Alone on the farm, Gary practiced groundballs by throwing against a concrete machine shed until baseballs totally disintegrated.

"Later, at only 14 and 15 years old, I started playing shortstop on the Maine All Stars. I was the youngest member of this men's amateur baseball team in the Countryside League. The players were usually much older than me."

As a 16-year-old 10th grader in 1964, he started at shortstop for Battle Lake High School and held that position until graduation in 1966. Harrington replaced shortstop Roger Olson who had graduated in 1963.

He also played shortstop as an American Legion player, member of the Battle Lake Lakers city team, Fergus Falls Junior College Spartans and for classic fast-pitch softball teams on the East Coast while in the U.S. Navy's nuclear power program. Harrington played shortstop for a military all-star team in Virginia Beach.

"Those groundballs off the ol' farm shed set me up to play infield for over two decades," he said. "The shed was bulldozed in the early 1980s, but the memories can't be buried."

He worked hard labor on the farm from about 13 years old right through high school, and also worked part-time for three other farmers in the area.

"I often wonder how I was able to haul hay bales all day in the heat and still find the energy to play American Legion baseball in the evenings," he said. "I guess I was just young and healthy."

He traveled around Otter Tail County on many Mondays in his early teen years with his father in a small cattle truck. They picked up livestock and returned to the farm, where they transferred the livestock into a semi-trailer truck that was driven to South St. Paul later the same day.

"I justly claim that not many people have been in as many different cattle and hog barns as I experienced," he said.

Today Gary and his wife, Karalyn, are happy to own and live on the farm site where he grew up. They have good memories of raising their two sons and ending their working careers in the Twin Cities.

Since 1978 the tillable acres on the farm have been rented out, contracted into Conservation Reserve Programs, or have been planted into trees or wildlife plots.

"We hope that in 2036 the farm will still remain in our family and might be eligible to become a Minnesota Centennial Farm," Gary said.

KARALYN HARRINGTON:
GROWING UP ON THE SCHULZ FAMILY FARM

Karalyn (Schulz) Harrington, who grew up on a farm north of Fergus Falls, asks the question, "Why is it that growing up on a small family farm in the 1950s and 1960s becomes more appreciated and valued as one ages?"

Her answer, "Maybe it is just being retired with a slower pace that affords time to reflect on the experiences, memories and life's learnings while being part of a farm family."

She says her farm life can be summed up by these themes: teamwork, sense of community, stewardship of the land, faith development and simple pleasures.

"Our farm was located five miles north of Fergus Falls, to the east of Highway 27 on a gravel road," Karalyn says. "The Schulz farm was a three-generation farm, homesteaded by my great-grandparents who left Germany in 1894 with four children from one year to 12 years of age."

They joined other family members who immigrated earlier, homesteading along the same gravel road in Otter Tail County.

"The living conditions in Germany were not good and the opportunity for common folk to own their own land in Minnesota was a huge draw," she said. "This led to stewardship of the land through the generations."

Karalyn's father, Walt, was born in the Schulz farmhouse and took over the farm in his adulthood. He died unexpectantly on the front yard, full circle of life on the farm he loved.

"My growing up in our neighborhood meant relatives, descendants of German immigrants, were up and down the road on every farm site," she said. "What a supportive neighborhood we had."

The Schulz farm was primarily a dairy farm, with a herd of 30 or so milking cows and young stock. Much of the crop production supported the dairy herd. The family had alfalfa for hay, corn for silage and grains for food and straw.

"We had a wide range of other animals," she said, "including horses, chickens, ducks, hogs, cats, dogs and wildlife. There was the dominating daily rhythm of milking cows in the early morning and again in the evening."

Walter Schulz as a young boy on his pony with the original foursquare farmhouse in the background

Walt Schulz as a young adult in front of the foursquare farmhouse

All other farm activities were done around the milking times.

"There were many jobs for my younger brother, Tim, and me," Karalyn said, "in order to help our parents (Walt and Lorraine) with the animals, along with a myriad of other farm responsibilities."

A special memory for Karalyn is the barn being a warm and cozy place to work during the winter. In the spring, summer and fall, an enjoyable job was walking out to the distant pastures to call (yes, they responded to being called) the cows back to the barn for evening milking.

Extensive gardening was a necessity requiring a team effort throughout the growing season.

Bringing the hay crop into the barn in the early 1950s

"We raised all kinds of vegetables and fruits, requiring countless days of canning and freezing produce. Filling the cellar, freezers and cabinets in the basement by fall was a huge accomplishment and source of comfort with winter coming." Building up a food supply included butchering, dressing and freezing chickens (which was one of her least favorite farm activities).

A sense of community extended beyond the immediate neighborhood to the country school (District 1430) which Karalyn attended through 6th grade. The 30-plus students came from several families, covering quite a distance.

The older students looked after the younger ones, which was important since there was only one teacher for all the grades. Parents, many who had attended the same school in their youth, were involved with the country school to make it a vital part of the community. There were programs, cake walks, meals, picnics, softball games, clean-up days, field days, etc.

"I loved country school, yet was ready for the transition to junior high in Fergus Falls," Karalyn said. She later graduated from Fergus Falls High School in 1967.

Membership in the Fergus 4-H Club provided another community of youth and their parents to learn and grow together.

"I was a 4-H member for ten years, with countless opportunities. I held club officer positions, showed Holstein cattle at the West Otter Tail County Fair and the Minnesota State Fair, participated in dress revues at the county and state fairs and presented a demonstration at the state fair."

"Winning purple ribbons at the Minnesota State Fair was a thrill, but spending four days on the Minnesota State

The Schulz Family
l-r: Karalyn, Walt,
Lorraine and Tim

The Schulz farmhouse with 1970s updates

Fair grounds and staying in the huge 4-H building with all the other Otter Tail County youth was even more thrilling," Karalyn said.

To this day, a stroll for her through the Minnesota State Fair 4-H building or the cattle barns brings on an attack of nostalgia. "Taking the long view, I feel 4-H played a key part in my personal development and eventual career."

"Developing faith on the farm came through traditional avenues including church services, Sunday School, confirmation, youth group and playing the organ for services as a teenager," Karalyn shared.

She emphasizes that living on the farm provided daily reminders of God's creation. Among them were the seasons, the animals, the weather and the landscape.

Faith was developed through the hard times. The crops hailed out in minutes, a highly-valued cow passed away suddenly, the chicken house was raided again by a deadly weasel, a combine broke down in mid-harvest, etc.

"Resilience, or the ability to bounce back, became possible through faith that things would get better," Karalyn said.

The phrase, "This too shall pass," served them well.

"Lastly, life on the farm was full of simple pleasures," she said, "among them swinging from ropes in the haymow of the barn and tumbling into the soft straw, riding a pony with no bridle or saddle, seeing full rainbows off to the east, smelling fresh cut alfalfa, letting the cattle out of the barn in the spring, sitting on huge boulders gazing at the surrounding countryside and distant horizon, and enjoying moments of absolute quiet."

Chapter Thirty-Six

Petterson Century Farm

by Joy Minion

OLE PETTERSON COMES TO MINNESOTA

According to information given to me by Vic Petterson, Jr., the Petterson's American history began with his grandfather, Ola G. Petterson. He was known as "Ole" or O.G. Petterson (the name he signed on his naturalization papers).

Ole was born on April 12, 1858, in Sweden. He served in the Swedish army before emigrating to Minnesota in 1884, locating first in Carver County where there was a Swedish colony. Wanting to learn the English language, he then went to Canada where he worked for the Canadian Pacific Railroad and later in lumber camps.

In 1887, Ole went back to Sweden to visit his mother who was ill. While there, he met and married Anna Jonsdotter Ise, and they emigrated to Minnesota, arriving in Fergus Falls on June 2, 1887.

FARM HISTORY

The original owner of the 160-acre farm, located in Fergus Falls Township six miles northwest of Fergus Falls, was a man named Taleck. At that time the farm was mostly woods, with only six acres of cleared land and a recently-built log cabin. The cabin had one room downstairs, an attic and a lean-to on the back. Ole and Anna purchased the farm in June 1887 for $10 an acre. Included in the sale were three cows, two calves and some chickens, the log cabin, a log barn and a hand plow.

Original log cabin with lean-to on Petterson farm

Ole walked to Fergus Falls to buy a pick ax and groceries. He then walked to a neighboring farm, where he bought a team of horses for $300.

The Pelican River meandered its way through the farm, and the cabin was located near the river. Native Americans frequently visited when Ole and Anna first lived on the farm, begging for food when they camped on the river, and Anna usually prepared something for them to eat.

When their first child was born (who later died in infancy), the Native Americans came to see the baby. For many of them, it was the first white baby they had ever seen. Ole said there was an old Native American who would come and play with the children every day, knowing he would be given something to eat.

*Ole and Anna
Petterson Family*

*Ole and Anna
(center front)
celebrating their
55th anniversary
in 1942*

Ole cut and sold wood in the winters, and cleared the stumpage in the summers. He received $1.50 for a load of wood poles, and $2.50 per cord for hardwood. There was a lime deposit near the river, and Ole often took loads of lime to sell in Fergus Falls. By the time Ole retired, he had cleared all but six acres of the woods on the farm. The original log cabin was torn down in 1928.

Ole applied for naturalization in 1887, and received his naturalization papers in 1900.

A new, nine-room house was built in 1897 (some records say 1903) on higher ground north of the old cabin, at a cost of about $1,700. A barn was built just east of the house in 1899 (some records say 1909). Carpenters at that time received $1.50 for a 10-hour day.

Ole and Anna had 11 children: George (died in infancy), Oscar, Minnie, Arthur (died age two), Alice, Arthur, Henry, William (died age 3 days), William, Charles and Victor.

Anna (born in 1867) died in 1947. Ole died in 1945. Both are buried in the Augustana Cemetery in Elizabeth.

Victor, born in 1908, married Ruth Peterson in 1933. He farmed the family farm with his father, taking it over in 1940 and residing there his entire life.

He was the Church Sexton of Augustana Lutheran Church in Elizabeth for 50 years. He also served on the church cemetery board for 50 years, and on the Fergus Falls Town Board for 35 years.

Ruth and Victor Petterson

Victor and Ruth had one son, Victor, Jr., born in 1939. Victor Sr. farmed until 1978, when "Vic" (Victor, Jr.) took over.

Vic Jr.

Young Vic attended School District #54 (as did his father and all of Ole and Anna's children). District #54 (later renamed District #1407), was located on Highway 59 just north of the present-day junction with I-94 and County Road 88. District #54 was organized in 1874 and dissolved in 1971. In later years, Vic owned the land on which the schoolhouse stood.

Abandoned District #54 school house 2007

After country school, Vic then attended Fergus Falls High School, graduating in 1957.

Vic married his high school sweetheart, Janet Torgerson, in 1959. While Victor and Ruth continued to live in the farmhouse built by Ole, Vic and Janet built a new home on the homestead in about 1959. They farmed Vic's home farm, raising crops and feeder cattle. They also dairy farmed until 2000. They had three children, Jon, David and Kimberly.

They purchased the farm in 1978, becoming the 3rd generation of Pettersons to own and live on the farm. They received the U of M Century Farm Family award in 1996. At that time, they owned and/or rented 600 acres.

Vic served on the Fergus Falls Town Board for 14 years, and sat on the Otter Tail County Planning Commission for 14 years. He worked with the West Otter Tail Crop and Forage Show for 40 years, and also participated in FFA, 4H and Ducks Unlimited. He was a lifetime member of Augustana Lutheran Church in Elizabeth.

Janet, a 1957 graduate of Fergus Falls High School, was an active member of Augustana Lutheran Church in Elizabeth

Janet & Vic Petterson

Dave, Kim and Jon

Dave, Kim & Jon Petterson

and served as organist for many years. She also worked as a travel agent, retiring in 2001.

Vic died in December 2012, and Janet died in February 2013.

The children all attended School District #1407 until its dissolution, then finished their school days in Fergus Falls. Jon graduated from Fergus Falls High School in 1978, David in 1981, and Kimberly in 1983.

Dave worked as night manager at Service Food for over 26 years. He also helped on the family farm, where he married Lanette Priem. He loved hunting and tournament fishing, was an active member of Ducks Unlimited and a lifetime member of the North American Hunting Club. Dave died in August 2009.

With two older brothers, Kim says she wasn't involved in the day-to-day farm operations. She said, "After I married and had my own two sons, I would bring them to the farm as much as possible and they loved it and seeing their grandparents." Kim married Jeff Lotzer, who is a chiropractor in Moorhead. They and their sons, CJ and Jacob, live in Fargo.

During high school, Jon was active in 4-H, FFA and farming with his family. Jon, the 4th generation to live on the farm, married Michele Johnson in 1992. An active Ducks Unlimited committee member, Jon was an avid outdoorsman who enjoyed hunting, fishing and trap shooting. He loved spending time with their two daughters, Autum and Lindsey, teaching them how to hunt, farm, and care for the farm animals. Jon & Michele built a new home east of the original homestead site, continuing to farm and raise cattle, besides working part-time for the Otter Tail County Solid Waste Department up until the time of his death in 2014.

After Jon passed away on June 5, 2014, the original farmstead went to Michele Petterson. Michele continued to crop farm for a couple years after Jon passed away, then chose to rent out the land but continued to raise beef cattle. Autum purchased Janet and Vic's house and 2½ acres in 2019, where she lives. As 5th generation Pettersons, both Autum and Lindsey still help with the cattle on the farm.

Michele says that one fond memory the girls have of the farm is the "wishing rock" overlooking the river in the pasture. "The story of its magic spans many generations," commented Michele.

Lindsey, Michele and Autum Petterson

Author Joy Minion's Note:
I lived in the old farmhouse built by Ole for five years from 2004-2009. Vic was a great storyteller and enjoyed sharing the history of his family and the farm with me. My thanks to Michele Petterson and Kim Lotzer for providing additional information and photos.

About the Author

Author Tom Hintgen is a Fergus Falls, Minnesota, native who graduated from Fergus Falls High School in 1966. He graduated from Fergus Falls Junior College, now M State, Fergus Falls, and from Moorhead State College, now Minnesota State University, Moorhead, where he majored in Mass Communications.

Hintgen worked for the *Fergus Falls Daily Journal, Fargo Forum, Pelican Rapids Press* and in public relations for Otter Tail Power Company.

His wife Sharon was administrator for the Otter Tail County Historical Society. She also worked at Lake Region Hospital and later taught math at M State, Fergus Falls. They have two adult sons, Mark and Paul.

The family has enjoyed visits and overnight stays at Itasca State Park, Glendalough and Maplewood State Parks in Otter

Tail County, and the North Shore along Lake Superior. They also enjoy hikes with their dogs, Maggie and Patches.

The Hintgen family deeply appreciates and supports the Otter Tail County Historical Society.

The author's favorite book readings have included biographies of people such as President Theodore Roosevelt, journalist Bob Schieffer, NBA star Elgin Baylor, TV star Johnny Carson, comedian Bob Hope, baseball legend Sandy Koufax and books by presidential historian Doris Kearns Goodwin.

Hintgen is the author of a 1981 book, *Baglien's Partisans*, which reviews the outstanding 1957 Fergus Falls High School boys basketball team. He also is the author of a book, *Golden Memories*, which covers life in Fergus Falls from the late 1940s to the early 1970s.

Hintgen and his family live in Fergus Falls, Minnesota.